The Dark Side of the Diamond

Gambling, Violence, Drugs and Alcoholism in the National Pastime

Roger I. Abrams
Richardson Professor of Law
Northeastern University School of Law

ROUNDER BOOKS

Published by Rounder Books

an imprint of
Rounder Records Corp.
One Rounder Way
Burlington, MA 01803

Cover design by Rachael Sullivan
Interior design and typesetting by Jane Tenenbaum
Photos Courtesy of National Baseball Hall of Fame Library, Cooperstown, NY

Library of Congress Cataloging-in-Publication Data

Abrams, Roger I., 1945–
The dark side of the diamond : gambling, violence, drugs and alcoholism
in the national pastime / Roger I. Abrams. — 1st ed.
p. cm.
Includes bibliographical references and index.
ISBN-13: 978-1-57940-156-6
1. Baseball — Corrupt practices — United States — History.
2. Baseball players — Drug use — United States — History.
3. Doping in sports — United States — History. I. Title.

GV877.5.A27 2007
796.357'640973 — dc22   2007028847
First edition

796.357
ISBN-13: 978-1-57940-156-6
ISBN-10: 1-57940-156-2
Printed in Canada
9   8   7   6   5   4   3   2   1

To Judge Frank M. Coffin, who taught me more than baseball.

Contents

Preface

Baseball is a pastime and a passion for many Americans. Writing about the vices of the game might be seen as heresy, but the game is more than a "gee whiz" phenomenon of American life. Of course, Albert Spalding, the premier entrepreneur of baseball at the turn of the twentieth century, could extol the virtues of the sport without qualification. He saw baseball as the "American game par excellence," but he acted as much out of self interest as personal devotion. After all, he was selling bats, balls and gloves.

These stories about the National Game will illuminate the dark corners of American life. There is no need to be cynical about either our sport or our country. It will suffice to be realistic and entertaining, by relating these tales of the game and the men who played it. Baseball has ably fit the American circumstance, the pastoral but urbanizing temper of the nineteenth century, the dynamism of the twentieth century and the technological context of today. It also showed us who we were as we changed with the times.

This book is the product of many hands and minds. My colleague from Rutgers University Law School, Marie Melito, was a careful editor and cheerleader, as usual. My wife of almost four decades, Frances Elise Abrams, read and reread every word to make the draft better. The folks at the Baseball Hall of Fame offered me the opportunity of a scholar's lifetime to use their 25,000 files of historical material to finish the book while serving as their Scholar in Residence. Rounder Books made the transition from manuscript to book as easy as a soft grounder to short.

Adrian Constantine "Cap" Anson, the nineteenth century's greatest superstar, stood "four square" against gambling, use of tobacco and alcohol consumption, as long as the sport banned all black ballplayers from the game.

Introduction

Well, it's our game; that's the chief fact in connection with it; it has
the snap, go, fling of the American atmosphere; it belongs as much
to our institutions, fits into them as significantly as our Constitution's
laws; it is just as important in the sum total of our historic life.
— *With Walt Whitman in Camden,* by Horace Traubel, 1906

The jury is impressed with the fact that baseball is an index to our
national genius and character. — Chicago Grand Jury Report,
November 7, 1920

FROM ITS EARLIEST DAYS, baseball has been lauded as America's sport.
On July 13, 1857, little over a decade after Manhattan's Knickerbockers
played the first game under the New York rules, the *New York Times* referred to the sport as "our national game." By 1867, after the close of the
Civil War, the *Times* would claim with confidence that baseball has
become "a permanent institution." Walt Whitman, America's poet, appreciated the coincidence between baseball and "the American atmosphere." He saw "great things in baseball." For a nation becoming
increasingly urban and congested, baseball would "take our people out-
of-doors, fill them with oxygen." Baseball, Whitman said, would "be a
blessing to us." Few would disagree with *Sporting Life* in 1884 when it
cheered: "Verily, the National Game is great!"

The Affair at Delmonico's

At a lavish dinner "served in nine innings" at Delmonico's jammed ban-
quet hall in New York City on April 8, 1889, the nation's business, cultural and political elite welcomed home to America the Chicago White
Stockings and a team of National League all stars from a goodwill trip
around the globe. At this "notable gathering of American manhood,"
the *Chicago Tribune* reported, baseball's "tourists" were "royally welcomed.... It was next to impossible to distinguish between the million-

1

aires and the athletes, and rich stockbrokers and gentlemen high in official life hobnobbed with the muscular ball thumpers." The 250 guests at
the Delmonico's dinner included Teddy Roosevelt, various business leaders and every important local politician. They regaled the athletes as
"representatives of American manhood and citizenship."

In his featured remarks that evening, Mark Twain likened baseball
to the American nation: "Baseball is the very symbol, the outward and
visible expression of the drive and push and rush and struggle of the rag-
ing, tearing, booming nineteenth century." Former (and future) president of the National League, Colonel A. G. Mills, lauded the tour for its
"contribution toward universal peace and good rule which Americans
have always done most to promote, and it stands without a parallel in
the history of sport."

As the nation neared the close of a century in which it had suffered
bloody internecine warfare, attracted millions of immigrants and transformed its economy into a mechanized juggernaut, baseball had
become a thriving urban business. Here was America's premier commercial entertainment. Although a citified diversion, baseball had always
tied itself to America's rural wellspring and pastoral myths. A successful baseball club would become the source of enormous local pride,
even though none of the players hailed from the locale. As the *New York
Times* wrote in 1888: "[T]he players are mercenaries who may appear
this year in the green shirts and scarlet stockings and blue caps of one
community and next year in equally kaleidoscopic raiment betokening
a new allegiance." Yet, the *Times* applauded the civic self-esteem that
baseball clubs engendered.

The Aesthetics of the Game

More than a century later, baseball has retained its central role in the
American panorama. It has become, as Thomas Wolfe wrote, "a part of
the whole weather of our lives, of the thing that is our own, of the
whole fabric, the million memories of America." Lyricists of the game
have long lauded baseball's unhurried elegance and classical aesthetics.

You come to the ballpark to share in the native experience, drink some beer, chat with neighbors and pass the time in relaxed tranquility. Robert Frost wrote with pride: "Some baseball is the fate of all of us."

Enthusiasts have always celebrated the spiritual qualities of the game. W. P. Kinsella wrote in *Shoeless Joe*: "A ballpark at night is more like a church than a church." Philip Roth agreed, calling baseball a "thrilling mystery...that reached into every class and region of the nation and bound millions upon millions of us together in common concerns, loyalties, rituals, enthusiasms, and antagonisms."

Baseball was "a good, wholesome sport" according to Walter Camp, the respected advocate for pristine athletic sportsmanship. Baseball was fit for every boy:

> It brings him out of the close confines of the schoolroom. It takes the stoop from his shoulders and puts hard honest muscle all over his frame. It rests his eyes, strengthens his lungs, and teaches him self-reliance and courage. Every mother ought to rejoice when her boy says he is on the school or college nine.

Fair play was baseball's great aspiration. Albert Spalding wrote in his hyperbolic memoir *America's National Game* in 1911:

> When two contesting nines enter upon a match game of Base Ball, they do so with the implied understanding that the struggle between them is to be one in which their respective degrees of skill in handling the bat and ball are alone to be brought into play, unaided by any such low trickery as that of cutting the ball, tripping up base runners, willfully colliding with fielders, and such dishonest methods of play characteristic of corner lot loafers. All these so-called "points" are beyond the pale of fair and manly play, and rank only among the abuses of the game.

Although Camp could preach idealized American values ("Gentlemen do not cheat [and are] courteous") and Spalding could boast about baseball's moral value, their countrymen knew better about their national game. Cheating had long been part of baseball. Nineteenth century professional baseball games used only a single umpire, and, when his eyes were turned, players on both clubs would take advantage of the absence of law. A runner rounding second base would head directly home if the umpire was attending to a hit in the outfield. At the same time, the shortstop would grab the runner's belt and hold him tight to the second sack. Ballplayers took advantage of the situation.

The men who have played the game at the professional level have not been saints, although there were a few, like Christy Mathewson, who deserved an elevated status in the pantheon of American heroes. Some ballplayers were alcoholics, others gamblers. Some were violent sociopaths. All were talented young male athletes, but they were merely human.

As a diversion from everyday life, baseball served as a welcome distraction. It was an amusement created for the public's enjoyment by fallible and, at times, dissembling human beings. Although appealing as an escape from the general humdrum of day-to-day life, baseball reflected the commonplace — what we are as a society, warts and all. It reflected all our human hopes and our venal sins. As *Baseball Magazine* reported in 1916: "Baseball continues to be the game where rich and poor, blooded aristocrat and husky immigrant, are on one universal plane." Baseball, it seemed, was congruent with life in these United States.

Barzun and Baseball

In 1954, Jacques Barzun, a Columbia University cultural historian, declared the existential lesson of baseball: "Whoever wants to know the heart and mind of America had better learn baseball, the rules and realities of the game." Barzun's aphorism suggests that there may be something unique about America that baseball might help explain.

Barzun's observation about the national pastime propels this inquiry. If we seek to learn about ourselves and our condition, we should examine our games, in particular the one game that for so long has affected so many Americans. The stories of the vices and bad habits of baseball will speak to us. Baseball has what Philip Roth termed "native authenticity." Some who do not appreciate the game may see it as simply trivial, a mere sport, a diversion. It may be much more than that. Baseball may be a microcosm of America, a mirror reflecting America with all its glories and all its flaws.

Barzun, who was born in France, was taken with the ideal of majesty represented by the game of his adopted land. Any witness of baseball will find his observations both true and familiar:

> Accuracy and speed, the practiced eye and the hefty arm, the mind to take in and readjust to the unexpected, the possession of more than one talent and the willingness to work in harness without special orders, these are the American virtues that shine in baseball. . . . That baseball fitly expresses the powers of the nation's mind and body is a merit separate from the glory of being the most active, agile, varied, articulate, and brainy of all group games.

There is more to both the civic and athletic portrait, however. Baseball offers a complex picture with many shades of grey.

The American experience is immensely complex and is filled with good stories and bad. Murderers, settlers, agrarian gentry, immigrants, political radicals, restless adventurers, business and labor organizers, and modern empire builders — depressions, recessions, prosperity, wars and peace, technological innovation and medical breakthroughs — it would be foolhardy to try to explain all these facets of a continental nation using the experience of just one of its forms of entertainment, even one as central as baseball. The task at hand is far more circumspect. Let us look to baseball for some information about America and its society, culture, business and mores. It is not intended to be comprehensive. After all, a mirror does not offer the viewer a full picture, only a two dimensional frontal view.

A Wondrous Game

Baseball writers and scholars have long acclaimed the beauties and spectacle of the game. Charles A. Peverelly wrote in 1866 in *The Book of American Pastimes*:

> The game of Base Ball has now become beyond question the leading feature of the out-door sports of the United States....It is a game which is peculiarly suited to the American temperament and disposition; the nine innings are played in the brief space of two and one half hours, or less. From the moment the first striker takes his position, and poises his bat, it has an excitement and vim about it...in short, the pastime suits the people, and the people suit the pastime.

It is fun to celebrate the many virtues of baseball. Before becoming buried in baseball's darker side, we should rejoice in the delight it brings to so many. Gerald Early wrote in *The American Poetry Review* in 1996:

> Baseball is, to be sure, an American cultural declaration of independence...the most active, agile, varied articulate and brainy of all group games....There is something about baseball's checks and balances that mirrors those checks and balances of the Constitution, of Enlightenment rationalism, or liberalism as a nineteenth-century ideology of organization and discipline, the great metaphor of self-interested individuals as self-interested association, the invisible hand of perfected design. Adam Smith as the Great Commissioner of Baseball.

No one has captured baseball's delights better than Roger Angell. In "Agincourt and After," reprinted in *Five Seasons*, Angell wrote:

> What I do know is that this belonging and caring is what our games are all about; this is what we come for. It is foolish and childish, on the face of it, to affiliate ourselves with anything so insignificant and patently contrived and commercially exploitative as a professional sports team, and the amused superiority and

icy scorn that the non-fan directs at the sports nut (I know this look — I know it by heart) is understandable and almost unanswerable. Almost. What is left out of this calculation, it seems to me, is the business of caring — caring deeply and passionately, really *caring* — which is a capacity or an emotion that has almost gone out of our lives. And so it seems possible that we have come to a time when it no longer matters so much what the caring is about, how frail or foolish is the object of that concern, as long as the feeling itself can be saved. Naivete — the infantile and ignoble joy that sends a grown man or woman to dancing and shouting with joy in the middle of the night over the haphazardous flight of a distant ball — seems a small price to pay for such a gift.

As Saul Steinberg, Angell's colleague at the *New Yorker*, wrote in *Time Magazine* in 1978: "Baseball is an allegorical play about America, a poetic, complex, and subtle play of courage, fear, good luck, mistakes, patience about fate and sober self-esteem." But that dichotic uncertainty is not yet the whole picture. Any human enterprise has blemishes and risks of corruption, and baseball is no exception.

Baseball became a commercial success in the nineteenth century because it attracted all classes of Americans as both participants and spectators. Upper-class Brahmins from Beacon Hill attended baseball games in Boston, as did poor Russian immigrants who sneaked over the fence to witness the national sport of their new homeland. Baseball was an action-packed, easily understood game with an appeal to all tastes. The working, middle, and upper classes found in the game a respite from ordinary life. It was a boisterous enterprise but within boundaries, a microcosm of the evolving American civilization.

At its best, baseball has played a positive social role in the community. In the 1890s, scoreboard boys would run through the urban neighborhoods announcing the game scores. Later, big electric scoreboards would be erected outside newspaper buildings and urban crowds would peacefully congregate to follow the progress of the local nine. As Mike

Burke, then president of the Yankees, said in 1971: "A baseball club is part of the chemistry of the city. A game isn't just an athletic contest. It's a picnic, a kind of town meeting." Burke told the CBS stockholders — CBS owned the Yankees — in 1969 that the clubs must show as much interest in the fans as the fans show in baseball.

On occasion, baseball showed us what the good life could be. Played on an urban island of green on a pastoral summer day, baseball offered welcome relief from quotidian burdens. The inevitable cycle of baseball from youthful spring optimism to the harsh realities of an aging fall reflected the universal human condition. From its earliest days, baseball was lauded because it was an outdoor activity: "We are too quiescent in our habits physically," bemoaned the *New York Times* in 1855. "Open air amusements" must be preferred. Barzun noted:

> Baseball teaches us about America's national character, wedded to timeless, rural, and individualistic values, although it began and flourished in crowded urban environments. Baseball as a narrative of American life is essential to the American biography.

The Dark Side

Even at a town meeting, however, there are deadbeats, delinquents, and malefactors. Some baseball players and fans have fallen into these categories. Baseball players have suffered from the same addictions and afflictions as members of the general public. It should come as no surprise that baseball players gambled. So too did (and do) most Americans. Some players were dishonest. In fact, the game itself countenanced chicanery within bounds, such as stealing a catcher's signs.

Sometimes we just accept cheating as part of the show. Gaylord Perry won 314 games and a place in the Hall of Fame by slathering the ball with Vaseline, although he was caught once and suspended for ten days. Whitey Ford, Lew Burdette, Don Sutton and Don Drysdale were also regularly accused of loading up the sphere before they threw it towards home plate. In the 1960s, the White Sox doctored boxes of baseballs to keep them from flying out of the park. In the 1980s, Dick Ericson, the superintendent of the Metrodome in Minneapolis, adjusted the fans and air currents in the domed stadium to aid the home team Twins. If they were losing in the late innings, Ericson turned on the fans behind home plate on high to assist the Twins batters reach the seats. Groundskeepers around the league regularly doctored the field to slow down or speed up runners and ground balls.

Batters have used every opportunity to advance their play. "Stormin'" Norm Cash admitted that he corked his bat the season he hit .361 with 41 home runs and 132 rbi. Many players — Graig Nettles, Pedro Guerrero, Dan Ford, Sammy Sosa, Andre Thornton, and Thurman Munson come to mind — have used illegal bats to enhance their performances. George Brett's famous "heavy pine tar" incident in 1983 has become part of baseball legend, although the presence of tar too high up on his bat did not assist his hitting. (Rule 1.10(c) of the Official Rules states that batters may apply pine tar only from the handle of the bat extending up for 18 inches.) As Steve Rushin wrote in *Sports Illustrated*:

> Cheating is to baseball as Bernoulli's principle is to fixed-wing aircraft: the invisible constant that keeps everything aloft. Hitters erase the back line of the batter's box; catchers "frame" pitches to induce called strikes; infielders occupy a different congressional district from second base when turning a double play; sluggers juice up on steroids till their forearm veins resemble bridge cables; and outfielders pretend that a one-hopper was in fact caught on the fly, holding up the baseball to the umpire like a prized tomato in a produce aisle.

Sports Illustrated, in 1981, reported that while coaching an all-star high school team Ty Cobb instructed his players on the finer points of cheating. Noticing that his catcher was playing within the rules, Cobb offered the following: "Here's a little trick for you. Just before the pitcher throws, grab a handful of dirt, and after he throws, flip the dirt up into the batter's eyes." Rogers Hornsby, perhaps the greatest right handed hitter in baseball history, wrote an article in *True* magazine in 1961 in which he admitted that he or someone on his team cheated in some way every game: "You've got to cheat. I know if had played strictly by the rules, I'd have been home feeding my bird dogs a long time ago instead of earning a good living in baseball for 47 years."

Some observers did not fully understand the finer points of the game played in full accordance with the rules. President Charles W. Eliot dropped baseball as a team sport at Harvard in the nineteenth century because he had heard that one of the Crimson hurlers threw a curve ball: "I understand that a curve ball is thrown with a deliberate attempt to deceive. Surely that is not an ability we should want to foster at Harvard." There would be few who played the game, however, who would mirror Woody Allen's professed naiveté. He confessed: "Whenever we played softball, I'd steal second base, feel guilty and go back." Pitchers regularly throw curve balls and no one goes back to first in baseball.

Some ballplayers have been violent, abusive and racist. Others were noble, honorable and dignified. Except for the fact that baseball players have always demonstrated truly distinctive athletic skills during their very short careers, nothing in baseball life is really different from American society outside of baseball.

Noted baseball historian John Thorn has written that "fundamentally, baseball is what America is not, but has longed or imagined itself to be." To the contrary, while these myths and aspirations are an essential part of the game, there is more truth to the assertion that baseball is reflective of what we are, not just what we hope we could be. Even though the game is just a form of entertainment, the character of baseball is, as Barzun perceived and Whitman and Twain described, the American personality, the American identity.

Cap Anson and America's Diversity of Identity

America is a land that generated myths to hold together its diversity of people. Its slogans were magnetic, even if only partially true. The Declaration of Independence promised rights that, in fact, would not be made available to most Americans. The free-market system offered economic success only to a favored few. The "land of the free" was not free for millions of African slaves. The home of democracy allowed only a small percentage of its adults to vote. Even among those entitled to vote, elections were bought and sold and preferences coerced by violence.

Baseball's place in the pantheon of American virtues also rests upon a canon of mythology that extols its heroes and their exploits. Examining the National Game might alert us to the function of mythology in American political and social life. At the Delmonico's all-star dinner in 1889 where Mark Twain waxed poetic about the national pastime, Chauncey M. Depew, then president of the New York Central Railroad, added that athletics like baseball were "the mainstay of civilization."

First in the hearts of the players assembled at Delmonico's in 1889 — at least that was the perception of the public — was the captain and manager of the Chicago White Stockings, Adrian Constantine "Cap" Anson, the nineteenth century's greatest superstar, the only player in that century to accumulate 3,000 hits. Anson was admired nationwide. A deeply religious Christian, Anson stood "four square" against gambling, use of tobacco and alcohol consumption, just the kind of man William Hulbert needed to represent his start-up National League in 1876. Hulbert induced Anson to break his ties with Philadelphia and join his own club, the White Stockings, for whom he would play for more than two decades. Anson played the game with flair and intelligence, but he could be a temperamental, nasty, pompous and sometimes cruel player. He was also thoroughly racist. In short, he was the embodiment of then current American virtues and vices.

In his brief remarks at the Delmonico's dinner, Anson said he was "thankful he had been permitted to assist in teaching the world what it most needed to know." Anson's primary lesson was already well known in the world, that white Europeans were a race superior to all others. Anson is credited with having forced the exclusion of black players from the major baseball leagues, and he did not hide his racist views. (Anson was an equal opportunity discriminator. He also hated the Irish.)

On August 10, 1883, Anson's Chicago team played an exhibition game against the professional club from Toledo, then in the Northwestern League. Anson refused to play if the Blue Stockings black catcher, Moses Fleetwood Walker, was anywhere on the field. Moses Fleetwood Walker, a bare-handed catcher, was one of twenty black professional ballplayers at various levels of the game in the 1880s. He played for Toledo when the club joined the American Association in 1884, the rival major league to the older National League. Moses's brother Welday joined the club for five games that season as well. Moses was only a fair hitter, but a good fielder. He had attended Oberlin College and the University of Michigan law school before playing the National Game professionally for five years at the Major League level. He was the last black player to participate at the Major League level for more than six decades.

The last black player to participate at the Major League level for more than six decades, Moses Fleetwood Walker was banished from the game as result of a "gentlemen's agreement" that reflected the prejudices of racist America.

The newspapers later reported that Toledo had no intention that day of playing Walker, who had a sore hand, but after Anson made such a fuss, the Blue Stockings insisted on Walker's participation. Threatened with the loss of Chicago's share of the gate, Anson agreed to play. (Money was always a way to convince racists to momentarily forget their twisted "principles.") Anson's Chicago club won the game 7–6, scoring two runs in the tenth inning. He then negotiated a clause in his 1884 Chicago contract that stated that no black ballplayer would be allowed to play against his team.

America's national policy had evolved by the late 1880s from one of post-Civil War equity to formal, oppressive apartheid. On July 11, 1887, the *Sporting News* editorialized:

> A new trouble has just arisen in the affairs of certain baseball associations [which] has done more damage to the International League than to any other we know of. We refer to the importation of colored players into the ranks of that body.

Three days later, on July 14, 1887, Anson's "no-blacks" contract pledge was put to the test. Chicago was scheduled to play an exhibition contest against the Newark Little Giants with their star black pitcher George Stovey. Stovey watched the game from the bench, and Anson triumphed. In a game at Syracuse, *Sporting Life* reported in 1888, Anson again "objected to [Moses Fleetwood] Walker's color" and this time a substitute catcher replaced him: "Anson will never pit the Chicagos against a team containing colored players." Within the next decade blacks were systematically excluded from professional baseball clubs at the major and minor league levels. The *Sporting News* could write by 1899: "Of course, the negroes do a good share towards supporting the game. But that is no reason why they should be allowed to take part in the game against white men." The color line was set firmly in America's game and in American society, where it would stay for decades to come.

Anson's prominent place in the history of segregated baseball was confirmed in 1900 when he wrote his openly racist autobiography, *A Ball Player's Career*. He described Clarence Duval, Chicago's black team mascot, in these terms:

> Clarence was a little darkey that I had met some time before while in Philadelphia, a singer and dancer of no mean ability, and a little coon whose skill in handling the baton would have put to the blush many a bandmaster of national reputation. . . . Outside of his dancing and his power of mimicry he was, however, a 'no account nigger,' and more than once did I wish that he had been left behind.

In his splendid new book on the baseball's 1888 world tour, Mark

Lamster describes one incident on board ship that encapsulates Anson's racism. When a fifteen-foot shark was sighted off the bow in the Indian Ocean, Anson suggested that they catch the fish using "little darkey" Duval as bait. The captain instead used salt pork, much to Anson's disappointment.

A bigot and racist of the first rank, Anson's views simply mirrored those of Americans. The formal segregation and subjugation of the freed slaves lasted for more than a century after their emancipation. To its eternal credit, baseball would later steer America out of this shameful legacy. When Jackie Robinson crossed over the foul lines at Ebbets Field in 1947 to join in association with a team of white players, America was led away from its heritage of hatred, bigotry and racism. Baseball, it seems, could both subjugate and liberate.

Baseball and the American National Character

As America approached the twentieth century, it would emerge on the international stage as a heavy hitter with a big stick. Francis Richter, the editor of *Sporting Life*, spoke of baseball and the American civilization:

> [Baseball is] a great sport, representative and typical of the people who practice it . . . one that stimulates all the faculties of the mind — keenness, invention, perception, agility, celerity of thought and action, adaptability to circumstances — in short, all the qualities that go to make the American man the most highly-organized, civilized being on earth.

Baseball was the exemplar of American commerce and triumphalism.

At its core, professional baseball had always been a profitable business enterprise. Shortly after the game became a leisure pastime in the mid-nineteenth century, businessmen set challenge matches to make money. They formed leagues, then colluded to pay their workers, the players, as little as they could. They restricted players from moving from club to club to eliminate competition over player salaries. They agreed among themselves on minimum admission prices, maximum player salaries, and exclusive territories. Baseball showed how American business succeeded.

Of course, these economic ploys of baseball's business leaders were likely in violation of the law, but the law was an annoyance to be swatted away like a fly on a summer's day. Although the Supreme Court in 1922 would rule that the business of baseball somehow did not affect interstate commerce and therefore was not bound by the federal antitrust statutes, state statutes and common law principles had long prohibited baseball's collusive reserve system and predatory practices. Fixing admissions prices and player salaries was blatantly illegal, but no one seemed to care. Violating the law to make money was as American as apple pie.

Sometimes baseball's blemishes became overwhelming, although we accepted them as part of the American scene. Ty Cobb, a violent sociopath, was immortalized as a legend of the game. He would exorcise his demons by spiking his opponents in order to injure them. He assaulted spectators who dared criticize his play and his character. "Baseball," Cobb said, "is as respectable as a kick in the crotch." Yet Americans adored him. When he jumped into the stands in 1912 at the Polo Grounds and pummeled a crippled fan, fans blamed the fan. The next day, the *New York Times* reported: "Cobb's execution was rapid and effective. Ty used a change of pace and had nice control. Jabs bounded off the spectator's face like a golf ball from a rock." Cobb was among the first players elected to baseball's Hall of Fame.

All fans know of the players on the 1919 Chicago White Sox who colluded with underworld gamblers and deliberately lost the cherished World Series. They were heroes to many, not felons. (After all, a Chicago jury of their peers had acquitted them of all charges after some of the players' confessions had mysteriously disappeared.) The Black Sox were not alone. There were reports that players on the 1877 Louisville Grays deliberately lost the National League pennant in exchange for payoffs. Players in the 1850s and 1860s took bribes to affect the outcome of games.

The faults of those who have played the National Game mirrored those who pursued other games in America — in business and in politics. Corruption, bribery, blatant violations of the law, violence in support of business advantage and other repulsive criminal activities have always been part of American life. While we have deluded ourselves into believing that we alone among nations stand for human dignity and equal rights, we are just part of a matrix of deceit.

Seamy behavior has always been a part of the baseball lineup. Henry Chadwick, the game's first chronicler, who earned the sobriquet "Father" Chadwick, proclaimed the sport's glories and exposed its squalor from the 1850s until his death in 1908. He responded to an 1881 editorial in the *New York Times* that had charged that baseball was a "sport unworthy of gentlemen," that indeed it was a sport that gentlemen did play as a "thoroughly national game of our own." He candidly wrote in the *New York Clipper*, however: "It cannot be denied that hippodroming [game fixing] has prevailed or that rum drinking as well as pool selling and gambling has prevailed on some prominent ball grounds of the country." A book like Jim Bouton's *Ball Four*, published in 1970, caused a great sensation even though it only revealed what insiders had known for a long time — the game had a very unpleasant side of alcoholism and drug use. The current scandal involving steroid use continues this long squalid tradition.

This book tells the stories of the unpleasant quarter of baseball, where conduct unbecoming ballplayers is too obvious and too important to ignore. These blemishes of baseball reflected the context of contemporary American life off the field. Alcohol and drug abuse by athletes mirrored our national psychopathy with chemical intoxication. The Black Sox scandal unfolded during a time of astounding political corruption. Petty violence, gross incivility, and rowdyism are cut from a single piece of cloth whether at the ballpark or beyond the fence.

Gambling by participants in the sport has been part of the game almost since its inception in the mid-nineteenth century. Baseball's most recent public *mea culpa* — Pete Rose playing Lady Macbeth, incapable of cleaning the stain of gambling off his hands — has become tragic public theater. Today, the sirens of illegal and performance-enhancing drugs have replaced alcohol as the greatest threats to the physical well-being of players and the integrity of the game, but the new ways to overindulge or to improve winning chances are just a continuation of nineteenth century dissipation and even, as we shall see, the early use of testosterone injections. Violence, often brutal, by players and fans has been a disturbing part of the game since its early days.

The Game Endures

With its ethical, moral and legal lapses, despite selfishness, pomposity, racism, and undiluted nastiness, baseball has persevered as Father Chadwick hoped it would. Individual excellence, achievement, selflessness and generosity of spirit still characterize much of the game. Baseball has a poignancy that can transcend its blemishes. Bart Giamatti, the baseball Commissioner who had too few times at bat, wrote about baseball in the *Yale Alumni Magazine* in 1977:

> It breaks your heart. It is designed to break your heart. The game begins in spring, when everything else begins again, and it blossoms in the summer, filling the afternoons and evenings, and then as soon as the chill rains come, it stops and leaves you to face the fall alone.

The sport's saving grace, of course, is that fans forget the pain, but remember the moments of glory — Bobby Thomson's home run, Willie Mays's over-the-shoulder catch, Sandy Koufax's perfect game and Jackie Robinson stealing home again and again. Its vices are of ancient origin, but the eternal virtues of the game ultimately triumph. Every season some, perhaps many, cities in the nation experience a rebirth of baseball mania. What goes on between the white lines is of first importance, but the rest of the story should also be told because it will tell us something about ourselves as Americans. Considered in context, the whole story of baseball will serve as a mirror of American life over the last century and a half.

By the 1890s, major league baseball performers, led by the feisty third baseman
of the Orioles John J. McGraw (shown here in later life as the illustrious manager
of the New York Giants), had fully adopted a street-fighting mentality.
"This parlor ball playing," he said, "doesn't go worth a cent."

Chapter 1

In the Beginning

Cheating is baseball's oldest profession. No other game is so rich in skullduggery, so suited to it or so proud of it. — Thomas Boswell, Washington Post

IN THE EARLY SUMMER OF 1858, thousands of fans came to witness baseball's first all-star game, a match-up between the best "ballists" of Brooklyn and New York City. Although Manhattanites may have been instrumental in creating what we now recognize as baseball, Brooklyn's amateurs clubs — the Excelsiors, Eckfords, Putnams and Atlantics, among others — perfected its play. New York too had its quality nines — in addition to the Knickerbockers, the Gothams, Eagles and Empires flourished in the 1850s. The hand-picked teams selected from all of these clubs had scheduled a best-of-three game series to establish preeminence in the world of baseball. They played at the newly-opened Fashion Race Course in what is now the Corona section of Queens. It was not an easy venue to reach. The only way from Manhattan was to take the Fulton Ferry to Hunter's Point and then the Flushing Railroad to Fashion Point. More than 10,000 spectators paid ten cents admission to gain entrance to the park, likely the first time admission was charged to watch America's new urban pastime.

The *New York Times* reported that there was "special provision made for ladies accompanied by gentlemen" and some 400–500 women attended. There was a festival atmosphere. "Mammoth omnibuses drawn by four, six, eight and ten horses were crowded with representatives of the various Base Ball Clubs, and were tastefully decorated with flags, banners and ornamented with streamers and bunting of various devices." No hard liquor would be sold on the premises, only lager beer, and no gambling would be permitted.

The match was a glorious spectacle. The reporter for the Porter's Spirit magazine gushed: "[N]o race day the Fashion Course has ever seen presented such a brilliant numerical array.... [T]he coup d'oeil...was brilliant in the extreme." Photographer Matthew Brady was there to capture the scene. Currier and Ives sent illustrators to memorialize the event. It was a genuine carnival of Americana.

A little over a decade earlier, New York City's Knickerbockers, a social and athletic club, had formulated rules for the bat-and-ball game that drew such crowds to Queens. Bat-and-ball games like baseball go back to antiquity. Drawings of women playing such a game adorned the Egyptian tomb of Beni Hassan in 2000 B.C. Writing to Marcus Aurelius in 150 A.D., Fronto, his tutor, referred to an argument between the two men and writes: "Malitiosam pilam mihi dedisti" which translates as: "You have bowled me a pretty dirty ball." Could it have been a spit ball? The English played a game called "club ball" as early as 1200, and pastimes such as rounders, one-o'-cat and town ball had been played by English and American children from the mid-eighteenth century. William Bradford chastised one of the colonists on the Mayflower for avoiding work to play "ball." Some sort of baseball game was played by soldiers at Valley Forge, by college men at Princeton in the 1780s and at Rochester in 1825. Rules varied from town to town. The games had various numbers of bases, using either posts or rocks, and any number could play. The bases were arrayed around a circle, square, diamond or triangle. The game of "base" referred to by the town ordinance in Pittsfield, Massachusetts in 1791 (together with "wicket, cricket, bat-ball, foot ball, cat, fives, or any game or games with ball") was just one of these predecessor pastimes and certainly not what we would recognize today as baseball.

This new game of the Knickerbockers would be different, however. Designed for young men with some free time who sought outdoor exercise after work, "base ball" would feature athletic skill, teamwork, formal rules and an umpire. The contest would be played by two teams of nine players, two fewer per team than the still widely popular British game of cricket that remained America's favorite pastime on the East Coast until after the Civil War.

Alexander Joy Cartwright, Jr., was charged by the Knickerbocker club he had organized to draft the first rules for their game, although the club had been playing practice games since 1842. The Knickerbocker club was to be an association of gentlemen amateurs, analogous to the Marylebone Club in England that promoted the game of cricket. Under Cartwright's Knickerbocker rules, that were formally approved as a by-law by the Club on September 23, 1845, order was brought to the game. The defensive players were arrayed around and beyond a diamond-shaped infield within foul lines (unlike cricket where the ball was in play if hit forward, sideways or behind the batter). A hurler on the defensive team would pitch the ball underhanded toward the batter, standing next to a round plate, who would strike at it and run. The distance from the corners of home and second and first and third was set at 42 paces. Thus, from the inception of the game the run from home to first base was almost precisely 90 feet. Flat bases replaced the posts or rocks. Circumnavigating the two other bases and returning to home base would score an "ace" or a run. The first team to accumulate twenty-one "aces" would prevail. This Knickerbocker version of the game, modified only slightly over the years, would become the most popular social and athletic diversion in American history.

On June 19, 1846, the Knickerbocker club hosted the inaugural baseball contest under its new rules in a game against former club athletes and experienced cricketers who were denominated the New York Nine. They played on a hot day under perfect blue skies on the Elysian Fields cricket pitch on the heights above Hoboken, New Jersey, then described as "the pleasure spot of New York." A canvas pavilion protected on-lookers from the sun, including the women who had made the journey. The exploding urban growth on the island of Manhattan had forced participants to leave their regular playing venue on the north slope of Murray Hill between Third Avenue and the railroad cut and take the Stevens Barclay ferry across the Hudson to find enough room to play. The fare was 6½ cents each way. Arriving on the Jersey side, the participants walked about a mile and a half up the riverside to an opening in the wooded forest. The Elysian Fields itself was a genuine country attraction, a "very delightful spot," according to the *Anglo-American Journal*. The heights above the Hudson are "certainly inviting," opined the *Christian Parlor Magazine*.

Cartwright offered to umpire the game and levied baseball's first fine, six cents "for cussin'" against a New York Nine player named Davis. He was seated in a chair on the first base line, although no balls and strikes would be called for decades. (Although there is no report about what Cartwright wore for that first game, umpires thereafter normally dressed in a frock coat and top hat and sat under a big umbrella to protect against the sun.) The Knickerbockers took the field in their new uniforms of blue pantaloons that were tight fitting at the ankle, "Hum brogan" shoes with wooden pegs as spikes to aid in locomotion, white flannel shirts, and straw hats. The catcher (or, as he was called then, the "behind") took his position thirty feet behind the batter. The pitcher delivered the ball straight-armed to the batter. The ball had a rubber center, weighed about six ounces and was ten inches in circumference, huge by modern standards.

Despite their sartorial splendor, the Knickerbockers lost that first game in four innings 23–1 against their former clubmates. After the match, the contestants indulged in a sumptuous, multi-course dinner at the nearby McCarty's Hotel. Within a very short time, word of this new game had spread, and letters poured into the Knickerbocker clubhouse seeking copies of the printed rules. On October 21, 1845, the New York Nine played a challenge match against a team from Brooklyn, the first recorded interclub game under the Knickerbocker rules. It would be five years before the Knickerbocker club played another outside team, this time defeating the Washington Club 21–11 in eight innings at the Old Red House Grounds in Manhattan. By 1857, 24 baseball clubs had been organized to play "the New York game."

The Elysian Fields hosted many athletic contests mid-century, but also experienced the racial violence that was characteristic of the antebellum North. Early in the morning of July 4, 1852, a black waiter at the Elysian Fields Hotel, one Charles Williams, was stabbed by Robert Canton, a 26-year-old Irish immigrant who had recently arrived in this country. The fight was over a job. Mrs. McCarty, the proprietress of the Hotel, had discharged all her black waiters and replaced them with Irish waiters. She found, however, that "they did not suit her customers and...she engaged the blacks to come again," according to the New York Times. This "gave great offense to the whites." Twenty young Irishmen revenged their loss of employment by attacking four black waiters with knives, sticks and stones. Williams, married and a father, cried out when stabbed: "Oh God, I am a dead man." Peter Ashley, one of the blacks, grabbed the attacker and held him down until the police could be summoned. Williams died twenty minutes later, and Canton was held for trial and later found guilty of manslaughter.

Then, as now, New York was a center of immigration, urban violence and the sports universe. The New York version of the new game of baseball would spread up and down the Eastern seaport, triumphing over the more complicated Massachusetts town ball version. The simplicity of the New York game spurred the creation of social and athletic clubs in Philadelphia, Baltimore and Washington to play the sport for "beneficial recreation." Amateurs who were dressed according to club rules would play games in the late afternoons from spring through fall. The Knickerbockers kept their distinctive uniform of blue woolen pants and white flannel shirts, according to Charles Peverelly, whose *Book of American Pastimes* in 1866 was the first to include a complete description of the new sport.

By 1858, what had started purely as an athletic diversion by white-collar working men with aspirations to be a social elite had evolved into a serious competition for local sporting pride. Entrepreneurs enclosed playing fields and sought to make money charging admission to spectators who came to observe the contests and cheer on the participants. The ballplayers of Brooklyn, New York's neighboring city across the East River, firmly believed they could beat the Manhattanites at their own game. Accordingly, they challenged their New York cousins to a best-of-three-game series. The Fashion Race Course tournament was the talk of the town, and it would determine true amateur supremacy on the field of play.

The first game on July 20 (rain had caused a postponement of the original July 13 date) was a spirited contest with some "extraordinary displays of good judgment and fine play," and the New York club prevailed 22–18. "The result was received with immense cheering," the *Times* reported. Refreshments followed. The second contest on August 17 brought the Brooklynites even with a 29–8 victory in "a most lively game." The *Times* noted that it was an extremely warm day, but a passing light shower "made it exceedingly pleasant."

The third and "conquering game" of the "Great Base Ball Match" was scheduled for September 10, 1858. New York prevailed 29–18. Even though Brooklyn's star player Masten was absent, the odds had favored the nine from the City of Churches. New York's batting, however, was simply "much better and more fortunate." The Brooklyn club was not disgraced, but New York emerged triumphant. New York took home the trophy, the ball that was used for that third game, appropriately gilded and inscribed. That ball is now on display in the Hall of Fame Museum in Cooperstown.

Much to the surprise of the organizers of the Fashion Race Course series, the ten-cent admission created a surplus of $71.09, which was donated to the widows and orphans of the fire departments of New York and Brooklyn. Although these proceeds went to charity, entrepreneurs quickly recognized that these baseball spectacles could be moneymaking activities. In addition to its potential for profit, the Fashion Race Course tournament also vividly demonstrated how, even during its very earliest days, baseball would have its dark side.

The Dark Side of the Diamond

The local press covered the Fashion Race Course event as a notable social occasion. It reported, to no one's surprise, that many male supporters of the Brooklyn nine had gambled on the game and lost significant amounts. The *New York Times* simply noted: "Space does not admit of descriptions of gambling, and cadging, and other delectable modes of making the dimes or dollars." It did report as a notable "scandal" that the women at the Fashion Race Course had made small wagers on the game. According to observers, local rowdies and pickpockets roamed freely among the onlookers. At times, the outmanned police in attendance lost control of the crowd.

Prior to the start of the third game of the Fashion Race Course series, two spectators placed a $100 bet on whether star player John Holden would hit a home run when batting against John O'Brien. The bettor who thought Holden would homer offered the ballplayer $25 were he to hit a round-tripper. Holden connected and he collected, as did his sponsor on the bet. For the first time — at least for the first time such an incident became public — gambling between fans had a direct and immediate impact on the outcome of a contest with a payoff to a player.

Within the decade to come, ballplayers would discover that they could sometimes profit financially by losing games in which they played. The first reported incident of throwing a game, what would later be termed "hippodroming," occurred in 1865. Three players on the New York Mutuals, Manhattan's leading ball club, accepted one hundred dollars each to lose the September 28, 1865, contest against the Brooklyn Eckfords. When their perfidy was uncovered, the club expelled Ed Duffy, William Wansley and Thomas Devyr from baseball. They would all soon be reinstated.

Albert G. Spalding's classic 1911 book, *America's National Game*, while an idiosyncratic history of baseball "with personal reminiscences of its vicissitudes, its victories and its votaries," dutifully records baseball's early vices as well as virtues. Baseball had flaws much like the rest of the American society that had adopted the game as its own. Spalding acknowledges that spectators were often ruffians, that players were morally flawed and that the exhibitions, at times, were fixed. "From the very beginning," Spalding admits, "betting had been openly, widely, almost generally indulged in at all contests of importance." Even more troubling, betting "begot collusion between those who bet their money and some of those who played the game."

The original members of the Knickerbockers club had hoped to retain an exclusive franchise on the new amateur sport for the better classes. If the sport was played only by private fraternities, the game could remain elitist and pure. Their plan, however, was destined to fail in a country that trumpeted egalitarianism over class status. Anyone could afford to play this new game, especially when the only required equipment was a ball and a bat. (There would be no real baseball gloves for decades, until Spalding began wearing one on the field and selling them in his sporting goods store in Chicago in 1875. One ball would last a full game or more.)

After the 1858 Fashion Race Course series, promoters realized that both the bourgeoisie and the proletariat would pay to watch the game played. Any person with the price of admission (or the guile to sneak over, under or around a fence) could observe a contest. Although members of the carriage trade had devised the original rules, athletic excellence knew no social class. A country seeking to establish its cultural independence from the Old World needed a "national" sport. The game of baseball, with all its glories and improprieties, would soon come to epitomize all of America.

America's Game

From its early days at mid-century, observers imbued baseball with all-American virtues. The nation's expanding influence and jingoism in the world required the definition of distinct and masculine American attributes. Baseball would serve well in this capacity as America's game. The team sport would also provide the outdoor exercise young men needed, and it would help develop the sense of social cohesiveness essential for the citizenry of an active nation.

At first some doubted that baseball could serve as a symbol for the American identity. *Harper's Weekly* wrote on October 15, 1859, that baseball had only taken root in a few coastal cities: "We see no evidence that either base-ball or any other athletic game is so generally practiced by our people as to be fairly...called a popular American game." As the country prepared for the Civil War, *Harper's Weekly* changed its tune. It commended the game as an admirable preparation for the coming conflict: "The Base-Ball Club has this great value at the present moment, that it is the 'school of the soldier' in vigor, endurance and agility." If this sport was to serve as the national game, then it deserved the allegiance of the citizenry, and the men who played the game had to possess the best of a distinctly American set of qualities — individualism, honor, virtue, morality, and freedom all wrapped in the Stars and Stripes. What the *Sporting News* called the "sentimental side" of baseball soon became the embodiment of all things American.

Baseball thrived as an urban, democratic game, and spread beyond the big cities. Porter's Spirit of the *Times* in 1856 related: "This is truly a national game [that] is played by the school boys in every country village." It was the training ground for young men who would have to defend American values on the battlefield. Although started as a diversion for urban white collar workers — merchants, clerks, journalists, and skilled workers — it soon served to prepare those who would fight the military battles to come. As the game evolved in the 1870s into a contest played by professionals for the entertainment of the paying public, baseball took on a social role as a societal adhesive. President Chester A. Arthur, upon receiving a delegation of ballplayers at the White House on April 3, 1883, exclaimed: "Good ballplayers make good citizens."

In the very beginning, Alexander Cartwright and his Knickerbocker compatriots appreciated the fallibility of man. The text of his original rules provided for a six-cent fine for the use of "profane or improper language," and, as noted earlier, Cartwright enforced that rule in the first game played under the Knickerbocker Rules. At any modern Yankee-Red Sox contest, that rule would result in a bonanza of riches for the sin tax collector, assuming the rule applied to spectators as well as to players. Later, clubs would impose fines on players who arrived for the games under the influence of alcohol. The *Cincinnati Enquirer* reported that pitcher Leon Viau reported for duty on May 28, 1889, with "a head on him the size of a brewery tub." Despite his alcoholism — or perhaps because it deadened the pain in his arm — that season Viau pitched 373 innings and won 22 games. At his death in 1947, Viau's obituary called

Baseball's premier entrepreneur of the nineteenth century, Albert Spalding saw the game as a "good, wholesome sport," plagued, at times, with sordid gambling, game-fixing, drunkenness and unruly behavior.

him "the fastest pitcher in the long line of Cincinnati's old-time hurlers." Viau, a handsome fellow, also played without a cap because his bushy hair would project from the bill and disturb his concentration. It was said that he always pitched his best ball on ladies day.

From its earliest days as a spectator sport, baseball attracted rowdies who would hurl epithets and beer bottles, rush the field and engage in scuffles. As Spalding recorded:

Liquor selling either on the grounds or in close proximity thereto was so general as to make scenes of drunkenness and riot of everyday occurrence, not only among spectators, but now and then in the ranks of the players themselves. Many games had fist fights, and almost every team had its "lushers."

Sitting out in the sun on "the bleaching boards" (later shortened simply to "the bleachers"), gangs of youths would engage in unruly behavior, a continuation of their off-field pastimes. The urban environment of the nineteenth century also bred social depravity. Cities were cesspools of refuse, both literally and figuratively. Police were rarely present, and life was dangerous.

Baseball's spectators seemed to relish this indecorous environment, however. They came to have a good time, gamble on the play and share in the joys of victory. By 1870 they could buy beer at the games, first at the Cincinnati Red Stockings grounds and soon thereafter at other baseball venues. The *Chicago Tribune* reported on August 15, 1880, that the captain of the Cincinnati club had been "ordered to slow-up between innings so as to allow the crowd to drink more beer, the profit on which was an important source of revenue to the Club." The *Tribune* opined that this relationship between alcohol and baseball was "degrading, offensive [and] ruinous" and should be banned by the League. With the addition of alcohol to the mix of potential mayhem, the police faced a greater challenge keeping order. Baseball's enthusiasts were not choirboys. A Syracuse newspaper described the game's spectators as "drunken rowdies, unwashed loafers and arrant blacklegs."

On the field, players would systematically bend or break the rules to obtain an advantage. Noted "ballist" Candy Cummings had developed the curve ball in 1867 by violating the rule that required the pitcher to deliver the ball with a stiff-armed, underhand motion. (Legend has it that Cummings discovered the curve by throwing clam shells at the sea shore.) "Sharp practices" prevailed in pursuit of victory on the field. By the 1870s, players on the benches would heckle the opposition without bounds, a breach of propriety and good sportsmanship that would have appalled the founding Knickerbockers.

The leaders of the game understood the human frailties of those who played the sport. A. G. Mills, the president of the National League between 1882 and 1884, recognized the highs and lows of baseball athletes:

> The occupation of a ball player is full of life and excitement. Each player is the hero of a certain circle of admirers, and he often finds hero-worship an expensive luxury. Ball players as a rule are generous and companionable. They have friends in all of the many cities they visit, and the frequency of opportunities and temptations to part with their earnings is not common to most other pursuits.

Club owners knew this about their ballplayers and often hired Pinkerton guards to trail them to monitor their off-field behavior.

By the 1890s, major league baseball performers had fully adopted the rowdies' street-fighting mentality that they thought would enliven play on the diamond. Pitchers, now hurling overhand, would throw "dusters" at batters' heads to keep batters away from the plate. Brawls were also common. John A. Heydler, an umpire during the 1890s and later president of the National League, described ballplayers as "mean, vicious, ready at any time to maim a rival player or an umpire, if it helped their cause."

During his playing days, John J. McGraw was foremost among the hooligans. McGraw was a repeat offender as the scrappy third baseman of the Baltimore Orioles of the 1890s: "This parlor ball playing," he said, "doesn't go worth a cent." His later three-decade managerial career offered him fewer opportunities for physical scraps, but he regularly would "kick" about umpire calls and received a full measure of ejections from the contests. His brashness and swagger mirrored the American ethos.

The early days of the game also had their paragons of virtue. One who stands out is Harry Wright, a worthy role model for generations of young boys. Born in Sheffield, England, Wright would be a leading figure in the American game for decades. In 1854, he joined the Knickerbocker club and learned the game that would be his life's work. At the behest of Cincinnati businessmen, Wright assembled the first openly all-professional team, the Red Stockings, that toured the nation in 1869, traveling 10,879 miles. Wright's club crushed its opponents by a combined tally of 2,395 runs to 574, with 57 wins and no losses. The club's share of each gate averaged a thousand dollars a game. Later Wright moved the club to Boston to field a consistently triumphant team for the five years of the National Association league. Finally, in 1876 Wright's Boston club, now called the Red Caps, joined the new National League.

Wright managed major league teams until leaving the game after the 1893 season. He would advise his charges about propriety: To make the grade a player should live "regularly," avoid late hours, tobacco and drink and "eat hearty — roast beef rare will do." He was an inspirational leader and a very successful businessman. Wright was an exemplar of baseball respectability.

The young men of baseball, however, came in all shades of morality — but, of course, not in all colors of skin. With the exception of a handful of black ballplayers in the 1880s, baseball at the highest level strictly enforced a sports apartheid that mirrored America's racist social and legal policies and practices. There is no particular reason to expect the men of baseball to be better than we are as a people, although, it should be noted, Jackie Robinson's heroic 1947 season as the first modern black major leaguer predated Truman's desegregation of the armed forces by a year and the Supreme Court's desegregation of the public schools by seven years.

Throughout its history, most members of the public would follow the game in the newspapers. Henry Chadwick told the stories of the game — both good and bad — almost from its inception. Writing for numerous New York City newspapers for almost a half century, Chadwick stressed the need for the press to be impartial and accurate. He recognized that the press was critical to the continued development of the sport. "It is the press," he wrote in the *Brooklyn Daily Eagle* in 1864, "that has made the game what it is, and it is to the aid of the press that base ball players should look to enable them to make it a permanent institution of the land."

The *Newark Daily Advertiser* in October 1865 waxed eloquently about how this new game could unite a heterogeneous nation:

> In that little republic of base ball, the child of wealth is seen playing with the youthful ragamuffins from some neighborhood alley, and the magic ball passes swiftly from the pretty hand of the patrician boy to the soiled fist of the little plebian. When, indeed, we see the general interest manifested among all classes in this manly and healthful sport, not only in our own city but throughout the country, we must acknowledge that it is rightfully called the National Game of America.

Such hyperbole about baseball was common in the nineteenth century and throughout most of the twentieth century. In the same way as the press often painted a rosy picture of the great American democracy as a blessed form of self-government suitable for all mankind, baseball writers bestowed on America's pastime an infallibility that was equally undeserved.

A more complete picture of baseball behaviors can tell us much beyond the heroics of a few fine athletes. It can tell us a rich story of a complex continental nation that was founded in liberty for some and slavery for others, that strove to find gold in individual achievement and in coordinated thievery, and that ultimately emerged on the world stage in the twentieth century as a boisterous adolescent convinced of its destiny. Baseball was our mantra because, in the minds of many, it symbolized a nation where joint effort and individual excellence were rewarded. It was also a game where rules were broken unless the umpires saw the transgressions.

We have always taken baseball way too seriously. Rev. J. T. Crane satirized the absurdities of the game in 1870 in his book *Popular Amusements:* "They pitch, they bat, they run, they pant, they grow red in the face, they perspire, they strain their muscles and rend their garments in superhuman effort." It is, he reminded us, only a game.

Baseball was designed in the beginning as a pure and healthy exercise and it has provided entertainment to the American public for a century and a half. Over that expanse of time, the game demonstrated the American character to its multitude of fans. We hoped that baseball would teach our youngsters about resourcefulness and fortitude, adherence to rules and authority, teamwork and pride. At the same time, however, it taught the next generation about partisan rivalries, violence, disparagement, cheating, and human frailty. It resonated with the full context of American society, and it has told us much about whom we were and whom we are today.

Gambling flourished at ballparks throughout the history of the game. These Royal Rooters for the Boston Red Sox traveled with the club, money in hand, to place bets on their favorites.

Chapter 2

Gambling on the National Game

"The gambling known as business looks with severe disfavor on the business known as gambling."— Ambrose Bierce

"BASEBALL," WROTE FRANK DEFORD in *Sports Illustrated*, "is historically hysterical on the subject of gambling." Baseball and gambling have always been a natural matched pair. Of all the available sins — and there are many — gambling has always presented the greatest threat to our national game. The hysteria is firmly based on baseball's long history with wagering and the associated threat of game-fixing.

Baseball proved ready-made for gamblers because of the indeterminacy of each game. The sport is a publicly observable contest played in accordance with well-defined rules. On any given day, every batter can succeed or fail and every club can win or lose, a precondition for an acceptable bet. Other than the progenitor professional club, the 1869 Cincinnati Red Stockings who barnstormed nationwide without a loss, most baseball clubs finish a season with many losses and many wins. Throughout most of baseball history, the best clubs might win two-out-of-every-three contests; the worst one-out-of-every-three. From its earliest days in the nineteenth century, the moment the gong sounded and the umpire directed the pitcher to throw the first pitch, no one knew how a game played "on the level" would end. Baseball games were thus the perfect subject for a bet.

Among club owners and league officials, there was always pronounced and regularly professed opposition to any gambling on the professional game. How else could it remain, as Albert Spalding wrote, "a good, wholesome sport?" Putting to one side the ever-present risk of thrown contests, gambling itself presented profound risks to the entertainment value of the enterprise. Here were great athletes exhibiting their skills at the highest level. It was the pitching, the hitting and the fielding that should matter, not the odds.

Gamblers, on the other hand, never focused their attention on the entertainment value of the athletic enterprise. They wanted a human lottery, where skill and chance produced unpredictable results. It was the outcome of the contests that mattered to them, rather than how it was achieved. To discount the athletic event as a roulette wheel was to undermine the spectacle and to risk limiting potential attendees to those who only came to gamble.

The *Brooklyn Eagle* recognized the corrosive effect of gambling on the game of baseball as early as the fall of 1864:

> First class matches, nowadays, instead of being meetings on the ball fields for recreation, in which good nature and fun are combined with the excitement of a lively game to create an enjoyable sport, are transformed into serious trials of skill between contestants who are, in one respect, but the mere automatons on a mimic field of battle, handled for the pecuniary benefit and personal interests of an outside class, who care no more for the game, as a means of enjoyable exercise and recreation, than they do for the improvement of the equine stock of the country by means of the race courses, their sole motive being the gratification of their gambling propensities, at the expense of a manly pastime and healthful exercise.... It is about time these serious, business-like contests should be changed to trials of skill, in which good humor and kindly feelings are the prevailing feature of the matches.

These were not hypothetical concerns. Only a decade after the rules of the game were formulated, a Mr. Morrow, serving as the umpire in 1857 of a contest between the New York Gothams and the Brooklyn Atlantics, was reported to have wagered on the outcome of the game he refereed. It was not fanciful to be concerned that his personal financial stake might impact on his umpiring duties. In 1884, Dan O'Leary, the player-manager of the Cincinnati "Outlaw Reds" club in the short-lived Union Association who always wore a carnation on his coat, placed bets on his club's games, but, as far as was known, he always bet that the Reds would win. (This was precisely what Pete Rose, the manager of the Reds over a century later, claimed he did — only bet on the Reds to win.) Players and owners openly placed bets during the first World Series in 1903. Perhaps it was gambling that was the national pastime and not the game of baseball?

Gambling in America

Americans have always enjoyed participating in games of chance. Gambling has been part of American life since colonial days. Risk-taking and speculation have always been indispensable to the American ethos and the source of invention and development. Throughout our history, millions came to America and took risks to get rich.

America essentially is a nation of risk takers, of immigrants who could have stayed in their home countries and accepted their circumstances. Instead, they ventured thousands of miles on a dangerous sea voyage, intent on creating a prosperous life on a new continent. Those who would call America home appreciated the fact that some would fail in this gamble. They liked the odds of success, however. They were not risk adverse, and they joined a nation of gamblers who embraced the uncertain future.

Religious leaders and social reformers railed against the sin of gambling. Wagering would lead to theft, idleness, delinquency and excessive drinking. It would undermine the moral values of society. It would foster secular passion instead of the God-fearing steadiness essential in a husband, father and provider. Early on, however, governments realized that the public's willingness to risk some money to win more money could be a valuable source of public funding. The Jamestown colony ran a lottery from 1612–1624. Starting in the mid-1740s, the Massachusetts Bay colony raised funds to pay its military debts through a lottery. The Continental Congress created a national lottery in 1776 to finance the

Revolutionary War. Benjamin Franklin operated a public lottery for the defense of Philadelphia "to defray the expense of building a battery below the town, and furnishing it with cannon." Lotteries raised the private capital needed to create Harvard, Columbia and Brown universities. By 1790, there were two thousand legal lotteries in the country. In his *American Notes* in 1842, Charles Dickens described a nation that was afflicted with gambling fever.

Lotteries continued to expand throughout the nineteenth century, leading the *New York Evening Post* to comment that "one-half of the citizens get their living by affording the opportunity of gambling to the rest." In 1867, the *Philadelphia North American* advised *New Yorkers* to rid themselves of those who engaged in "thieving, gambling swindling, outrage, vending lottery policies, keeping low dens of vice and iniquity, and election bullies and cheats." (There is no evidence New Yorkers listened to this advice.) The Georgia legislature enacted a special law in 1866 to allow lotteries to raise money for orphans of Confederate soldiers, and an exemption for this purpose was embodied in the state's Reconstruction Constitution of 1868.

Colonial gentlemen in Virginia were particularly passionate about playing their odds, and gambling was a core component of their sports culture. By owning slaves whose labor increased their masters' wealth, the men of the elite class were freed from quotidian tasks and could pursue the amusement of competitive gaming. They played whist and other card games, pastimes combining both skill and luck. They raced their horses, risking their reputations and social standing on their wagers.

The American Southern aristocracy saw gambling as a privilege of class. In a country where the class structure was mutable, however, financial criteria rather than patrimony determined status. The upper class could not effectively bar entry to those who successfully met the capital entrance requirements. By offering the opportunity for later arrivals to profit in America, members of the patrician class stilled calls for social upheaval that plagued their counterparts in Europe. There would be no need to guillotine your betters when, with good fortune, you could become one of the betters yourself.

Gambling also satisfied the American penchant to pursue shortcuts to financial success. Skills, effort, good fortune, and a willingness to bend the rules paved the way. Gambling offered the easiest route to wealth, one that Americans eagerly pursued. Gambling was engrained into the nation's laissez-faire economic system. Entrepreneurs who speculated in trading ventures accepted risk, as did the immigrants who wagered a few pennies on the roll of street dice. Both were gambling their assets in an uncertain environment seeking the big payoff.

For working class Americans, saloons, clubs, and community gathering places offered easily accessible venues in which to place a bet. Industrial boardrooms offered similar settings for entrepreneurial risk-taking without challenging Victorian sensibilities. Gambling in business ventures was not deviant behavior; it was all-American. The country's expanding economic base, especially after the Civil War, provided abundant opportunities to risk capital.

Both gamblers and entrepreneurs sought out opportunities for wagering and investing. Obviously, gamblers found that card playing and other similar activities were fit for this purpose, but for the "sports," a sometimes pejorative appellation applied to gamblers in the nineteenth century, other prospects were needed. Sporting men avoided regular employment and devoted themselves to gambling in various forms. Horse racing and prize fighting were full-blooded activities worthy of the gamblers' pursuit. "Pedestrianism," as distance speed walking was called, offered another wagering opportunity and attracted huge crowds in America. Cock-fighting had long appealed to upper-class gamblers in England, and it was transplanted to America to serve all classes as the basis for a bet in the back rooms of the ubiquitous saloons. At the end of the nineteenth century, gamblers also wagered on short-distance running, cycling, billiards, rowing, shooting, skating, swimming, wrestling, and, of course, baseball. Gambling was a business that made money, and, as such, it was perfectly American.

Even the most benign forms of gambling were subject to chicanery. Lottery privateers, unregulated by any governmental entity, would extract their profits from the pot before rewarding any of the winners.

Some lotteries were simply frauds with no winners except the man on his way out of town with the proceeds. A grand jury in New York in 1830 reported: "Lotteries, as now managed, are an evil of the most alarming nature, both in a moral and pecuniary point of view." Louisiana politicians in 1883 complained that "lotteries are not only inciting breaches of faith and embezzlement, but are demoralizing society, corrupting politics, and impeding legislation." They blamed Northern carpetbaggers for importing sin and urged that lotteries be suppressed. But despite these moral protestations, lotteries flourished across the country.

Gambling was a manly, assertive activity open to all with even modest resources, a perfect diversion for Americans eager to displace bourgeois and religious values with genuine individual autonomy. Gambling appealed particularly to nineteenth century immigrants. Put to work to build industrial America, working-class men found a sense of independence in gambling that they did not enjoy during their long hours on the job. Taking risks and competing against others seemed to validate their masculinity and individuality. They sought out opportunities to gamble on anything.

Urban reformer Jacob Riis correctly observed: "Gambling is by instinct and nature brutal, because it is selfishness in its coldest form." That was an essential part of its attraction, and winners suffered no social ostracism as a result of their successes. In fact, quite the opposite was true. Successful card players, like Wild Bill Hickok in the 1880s, were canonized as folk heroes. Captain William W. Williamson, a professional gambler, was elected chief of police by the voters of Mobile, Alabama.

At the same time that gambling offered the opportunity to get rich quickly, the pastime also relieved the boredom of urban life and the isolation of rural life. In a nation that was overwhelmingly peopled by rural farmers, gambling created a secular social web. In the cities, employees who worked long hours six days a week under dangerous conditions found in gambling a diversion from the dreadful sameness of their lives. They would engage in "policy gambling," lotteries with a daily drawing that would run in their neighborhoods. The same was true of the upper class, although the diversion for them was from the ennui of idleness. In *House of Mirth*, Edith Wharton's novel of upper-class life and values in the nineteenth century, gambling at cards served as an essential amusement for the elite. Lily Bart, her novel's protagonist, loses $300 one evening gambling at bridge, which leads to her ultimate downfall.

Gambling also produced tragedy, especially for the families of the losers. "The gambling habit of the American people," the *Chicago Tribune* wrote in 1883, must be counteracted "to save money for a class of people who have none to throw away." When a gambling pastime became an obsession combined with alcoholism and debauchery, it degraded the social community. Moderation, for which Benjamin Franklin had preached in colonial times, was only an aspiration rather than a reality.

Although state and local governments might try at times to abate private gambling activity that might compete with their own official lotteries, gambling generally was left uncontrolled by the authorities under prevailing laissez-faire regimes. Americans had long been skeptical of government's influence in their private affairs. The first national compact, the Articles of Confederation, offered the central government so little power that it fell of its own light weight in a peaceful coup at the Constitutional Convention in Philadelphia in 1787. Even then, the federal government would have limited powers. For most of American history, effective power was in the hands of private organizations, churches and civic groups. Maintaining public morality proved a major undertaking and was achieved with only intermittent success.

Baseball, Gambling and the Work Ethic

The nineteenth century was a time of boundless industrialization in America, and capitalists were rightfully concerned about the danger to the work ethic posed by widespread gambling among members of their workforce. Combined, as it often was, with excessive consumption of alcohol before, during and after wagering events, gambling undermined the core attributes of the steady workers needed in the industrial system.

Widespread gambling also risked the cardinal value of respectability that held society together in the Victorian era. As Thorsten Veblen wrote, gambling converted hard-working men into "lower-class delinquents." The Protestant church attacked gambling as the devil's work. The Kingdom of God lay waiting only for those who followed the paths of righteousness throughout their lives, and gambling was a troubling detour. On April 4, 1905, the Presbyterian synod, meeting in Missouri, condemned baseball as one of the "avenues to gambling." Religious leaders joined together to castigate temporal rewards unrelated to any spiritual undertaking. They also appreciated the importance of stability in society and worked with business leaders to imbue the multitudes with the values needed to support a stable religious and commercial social system.

Nonetheless, gambling flourished in America and, in particular, in the baseball environment. The report of the contest between the New York Mutuals and the Brooklyn Atlantics on August 3, 1865, extolled the virtues of the game which offered many opportunities for bets of $100 against $40 on a Mutual victory. (The Atlantics triumphed 13–12, however.) A letter to the *New York Times* in 1867 complained about the "large sums. . . . staked upon every game played by popular clubs." Everyone, or so it seemed, participated in betting pools, from the magnates of the game to the young boys who manned the refreshment stands under the grandstand. They would bet on the games, the innings, even a player's plate appearance or a pitch. They would select innings at random and win when the combined total of runs scored by both teams in that inning was the highest of the game. At the ball grounds, the third base pavilion often became the favored betting parlor. By the end of the nineteenth century, telegraph companies had connected the ball grounds to betting establishments nationwide, instantly distributing game results. This new technology facilitated gambling mania away from the site of the baseball game.

Beginning in the 1850s, only a decade after the game was formulated and even before the players openly declared themselves professionals, the nation's newspapers began reporting the bets made, won and lost by gamblers. The *Troy Budget* of upstate New York bemoaned the extent of the gambling madness, finding it "lamentable":

> It pervades all classes. At the game played with the Mutuals on Tuesday women brought their money and bet on their favorite Haymakers to the last cent in their possession. We hear of Lansingburg sewing girls who sent down their five, ten, and twenty dollars each by male friend to bet on the Haymakers.

As America's only regularly played team sport, betting on baseball became the preferred topic of conversation not just of professional gamblers, but also of members of the middle and upper classes — both men and women. It had been hoped that enticing women to attend the contests would abate the wagering. Instead, it simply created another group of gamblers. From early spring to late fall, many otherwise respectable citizens who would never play cards or shoot dice would openly wager on the outcome of the amateur and professional baseball contests that seemed to be everywhere.

As early as 1858, the National Association of Base Ball Players, a loose confederation of amateur ball clubs, formally banned betting by players, umpires and scorers. A violation of this cardinal rule would result in a participant's banishment from Association games. To enforce its prohibition, the Association used a blacklist. No Association team could field a banned player. Any team that played against a club that fielded a banned player would be contaminated and, as a result, be banned from Association play. This rule, of course, did nothing to stop gambling by fans, and it also did very little to stem the tide of gambling by players. The rule was universally ignored.

During lulls between the battles of the Civil War, Union soldiers often played baseball games and gambled on their outcomes. Many soldiers carried a baseball bat and a ball to war in their knapsacks. John G.B. Adams of the Nineteenth Massachusetts Regiment reported that while his unit was encamped in Falmouth, Virginia in 1863 "base ball fever broke out." Playing baseball reinforced the essentials of teamwork that were critical during a battle. It also offered soldiers the exercise they needed to stay fit. To enhance interest, prize money was set aside for the victors.

By comparison, the ever-present card games in the Civil War only separated soldiers from their Union greenbacks and Confederate blue-backs. Soldiers invented other ingenious ways to lose their money. Their parasitic body lice offered a unique opportunity to gamble on a race be-tween two insects placed in the middle of a tin plate. Accompanied by the cheers of the faithful, the "runners" would race for the edge of the "track." The first to fall off the plate was declared the winner and all bets were paid. More importantly, baseball, cards and even lice diverted the soldiers' attention from the terror-filled battles that lay ahead.

There were substantial risks in playing baseball during a war, how-ever. George Putnam, a Union soldier stationed in Texas, remembered a disastrous game played between the lines of the opposing armies:

> Suddenly, there came a scattering fire of which the three out-fielders caught the brunt; the center field was hit and was cap-tured, the left and right field managed to get back into our lines. The attack... was repelled without serious difficulty, but we had lost not only our center field, but... the only baseball in Alexan-dria, Texas.

Confederate soldiers held as prisoners of war learned the rules of the Knickerbocker version of the game from their Northern captors. While held at Northern prisons, such as the large facility at Johnson's Island in Ohio, Confederate soldiers would bet on the outcome of the games be-tween their compatriots. Upon the conclusion of the conflict, veterans returned home to spread the gospel of the sport with its accompanying wagering.

The pre-war baseball matches between amateur teams continued un-abated in the North during the war among those young men who avoided military service either by feigning incapacity or paying a $300 bounty. The fans and the gamblers followed these contests avidly. After the war, baseball and gambling continued to expand along parallel lines. Urbanization facilitated gambling, while baseball grew in stature as the national game. Newspapers continued to regularly report the terms of the wagers made at the games. In 1867, the *Newark Daily Advertiser* described the gamblers roaming the sidelines of an Athletics-Atlantics contest where men, "with their hands full of greenbacks, were walking around the skirts of the crowd calling for takers of bets at a hundred dollars to twenty that the Athletics will beat [the Atlantics] two to one."

Although the press facilitated the growth of the sport and the gambling that accompanied it, newspapers bemoaned the connection between gamblers and the national game. In 1864, the *New York Clipper* rued the very presence of gamblers at the games: "[A] class of individuals are introduced among the patrons of the game, and an objectionable influence brought to bear thereby, that seriously conflicts with the best interests of base ball, these influences being mainly such as...would bring the game down to a very low level." In 1869, the *New York Times* editorialized that baseball was in danger: "We are sorry to hear the current stories relating to the enormous sums which are said to have changed hands in betting upon the exciting games of base ball which have recently taken place between a western nine [the Cincinnati Red Stockings] and the championship clubs of New York and other Atlantic cities."

Although baseball began as a purely amateur pastime, in due course city and neighborhood clubs hired "ringers" to enhance their local nine's chances. The 1869 openly professional Cincinnati Red Stockings, sponsored by Queen City businessmen, caused a sensation as it toured the country without suffering a defeat. There was one tied game, however, against the Troy, New York, Haymakers, the result, reportedly, of gambling. Haymakers owner John Morrisey had placed a $60,000 bet on the contest. With the game tied in the sixth inning, Morrisey ordered his club off the field to avoid the possibility of losing his bet. The *New York Times* offered: "[N]o measures were too disgraceful for their backers to attempt in order to win their money, or, failing in that, to save it." In fact, gamblers offered bribes to the Cincinnati ballplayers "to induce them to lose the game." The *Troy Times* replied that the rulings of the umpire had been "unjust and outrageous" and that "fully justifies the action of the club in withdrawing from the field." The Red Stockings, according to the local press, had been "dishonorable and cowardly" and should therefore have made an "ample apology for the dishonor they have cast upon the game."

The Risks of Gambling

Gambling in America had thus become a formally improper, but tacitly accepted, social practice. Much like baseball, it was a pastime that traversed all levels of society. Unlike some other vices, especially addictive alcoholism and drug abuse, most participants in gambling exercised free will in deciding whether to participate. The social impropriety of the practice might even have enhanced its attractiveness, especially during the Victorian era when public decorum was mandated. The baseball entrepreneurs who staged contests upon which bets were made found the popularity of their enterprise enhanced by gambling, although that sweetener contained poison. Would spectators who attended games only to gamble drive away those who might attend simply to enjoy the spectacle of great athletes performing?

And what about the integrity of the spectacle itself? Gambling required that a game be on the level. To provide a legitimate basis for a wager, it was essential that the outcome of contests be genuinely uncertain. It was not a gamble to toss loaded dice that would come up with predetermined spots. If you knew it was already arranged that one baseball club was going to win, there would be no risk, no uncertainty and no basis for a bet. Even with the best of odds, no one would risk money on a certain loser.

The *Washington Post* on October 29, 1911, explained how the popularity of the national game depended on its integrity:

> When they say that virtue is its own reward, they do not refer to baseball. Not necessarily. When bankers, merchants, physicians, ministers, lawyers, professors, chauffeurs, laborers, office boys, and chorus girls to the aggregate number of perhaps 40,000,000

pay admission in the course of one season to the ball parks of the United States of America, those in charge of the sport find that honesty is remunerative, lucrative — nothing less, in fact, than a big paying proposition. . . . Baseball barons of the present day have become such because the public believes the national game is conducted on the principle of a fair field and no favor.

From the beginning, however, there was always the possibility that participants in the sport could throw a game, especially at a time when players themselves openly bet on the outcomes. Although Americans loved to take risks, who would not rather bet on a sure thing? Ballplayers were modestly paid, a far cry from the multi-million dollar salaries of the twenty-first century. The payoff from a fix for the player would be substantially more than that player's regular compensation, even discounting for the risk of being caught, which was minimal. Although idolized by fans of the game, ballplayers shared all their human frailties, including their insatiable desire to make a buck.

While the legitimacy of the sport and gambling required that a game be on the level, gamblers shared a weakness for a sure thing in the short run. Although in the long run honesty kept the odds business going, money was made in the short-run. Gamblers sought inside information on the physical condition of the day's hurler or the premier batter. Purchasing an outcome by encouraging a player to toss the game away through payment of a bribe would be even better. It would not have been unusual to find players and gamblers having a drink together at the neighborhood saloon. For gamblers, affinity with ballplayers could mean ready money, and the potential advantage was mutual.

During the nineteenth century, hippodroming, a conspiracy to throw a professional baseball contest, was a potent threat to the viability of the game both as entertainment and as a subject for a bet. At times, the prospect of a thrown contest placed the very existence of the sport in doubt. The *Cincinnati Gazette* even offered in 1879: "The baseball mania has run its course. It has no future as a professional endeavor."

Pool Selling

"Pool selling" was a particularly popular part of the nineteenth century baseball gambling experience. A scheme borrowed from horseracing, pooling the bets of gamblers made gambling safer and efficient. Direct betting between gamblers might result in disagreements when the losing party later denied entering into the wager or when questions arose as to the terms of the bet. Pools involved a middleman who auctioned options to bet on a club, taking odds. The pool seller would hold the cash (of which he kept a small percentage as his take) and pay off all the winners. This way no one could default on a bet. The first time pool selling, this "feature of turf meets," reportedly was used at a baseball game was at a match between the New York Mutuals and the Rockford, Illinois, Forest Cities on June 1, 1871, a contest held at the Union Ball Grounds in Manhattan. Three seasons later, the Union Ball Grounds would ban pool selling, but the edict was difficult to enforce.

Pool selling was an object of particular scorn for those who wanted to keep the national game free of the influence of gamblers. Baseball scribe Henry Chadwick bemoaned this practice as a degradation of the sport. Chadwick was concerned that pool selling enhanced the risk that ballplayers would fix the games in which they played:

> Unfortunately . . . this pool-selling innovation has proved more damaging in its results than any one dreamed of. . . . [N]ow the amount of money pending in a contest on which pools have been sold can be known . . . to a dollar, and hence the temptation to fraudulent arrangements for losing matches for betting purposes becomes so great as almost to be irresistible.

Pool selling on the ball field, Chadwick reasoned, was "demoralizing in the extreme." Even when games were on the level, the suspicion remained that they were not. Years later, Albert Spalding would write "that curse of all field sports, pool gambling, got its deadly grip on professional Base Ball, and brought it almost to death's door."

Pool sellers established betting booths at park entrances. The Brooklyn Atlantics' Union Grounds, the first enclosed ballpark, had a section known as the Gold Board where the pools did a lively business during games. In some cities "pool rooms" were opened away from the ball grounds at local parks, especially on those occasions when owners banned gamblers from the park. The term "poolroom" originally did not apply to a variation of the game of billiards. It dealt with betting "pools" of money.

Rather than corrupt the game, however, most pool sellers operated in a merit-based environment. It was in the pool seller's interest to make sure that the games were played on the level. Otherwise, customers would be reluctant to place their bets on a game where the outcome was suspect or predetermined. Individual pool sellers attempted to maintain a reputation for fair dealing. They were not angels, of course, and the specter of corruption and manipulation could not be easily erased. As a regular matter, losers in these pools alleged they were the victims of game fixing. The sale of alcohol at the games only abetted the ever-present risk of fan rowdyism generated by gambling.

Betting and game fixing plagued the National Association throughout its five years on the national scene from 1871–1875. Every error in the field was subject to suspicion. Was that a deliberate miss or merely an honest misjudgment of the ball's path? The *Chicago Tribune* in 1875 asked: "What is Wrong with Base Ball?" Game-fixing was the answer, or so the newspaper concluded. In 1876, the *New York Clipper* reported: "Any professional base ball club will 'throw' a game if there is money in it. A horse race is a pretty safe thing to speculate on in comparison with an average ball match." The connection between gambling, baseball and game-fixing would become firmly established in the public's mind as a result of the 1919 Black Sox scandal. As we shall see in the next chapter, it had its origin decades earlier during the adolescent years of the organized sport.

Gambling During the First World Series

At the beginning of the twentieth century, baseball was firmly entrenched on the national scene from spring until fall, and gambling was a well-known and accepted part of the enterprise. Players openly bet on games in which they played.

The *Sporting Life* reported on May 3, 1902, without editorial comment or criticism:

Ball Players Want to Gamble.

The members of the Pittsburgh baseball team have made up a pool of $10,000 to wager that they will win the National League pennant this season. This action was provoked by a reported announcement by Frank de Haas Robison, of St. Louis, that he would put up $10,000 against Pittsburgh winning the flag. The Pittsburgh players at once accepted the deal and wired Mr. Robison today that his challenge had been accepted.

The Pirates won the pennant that year by 27½ games over Brooklyn.

The men who ran baseball at the turn of the century appreciated the potential damage gambling could do their sport. The President of the American League, baseball's strongman Ban Johnson, issued an order on August 17, 1903, forbidding betting at American League ballparks. Earlier that year, however, Johnson had approved a well-known New York bookie, Frank Farrell, as one of the owners of the New York Highlanders franchise relocated from Baltimore. Johnson had plainly stated his intention a few years earlier to offer a clean sport to the patrons of the game. Although Johnson was a remarkably successful entrepreneur who created the rival American League and bested the National League in economic warfare, he could not rid the game of gambling.

The sporting pages of every newspaper carried evidence that Johnson's edict was simply ignored. Gamblers were all over the game. During the first modern World Series played in 1903 between the Boston Americans and the Pittsburgh Pirates, the newspapers featured stories about the wagers placed by the fans, the players and the owners. The series, planned by the owners of the two pennant-winning clubs as a best-of-nine tournament, featured splendid pitching, stalwart hitting and abundant gambling. When the Pirates traveled from the Smoky City of Pittsburgh to the Hub of Boston for the first three games, their loyal gamblers accompanied the club aboard the players' special train. Ensconced on the ground floor of the Vendome Hotel in Boston's Back Bay, the Pittsburgh sports met with their Boston counterparts to lay odds on the outcome of the contests. The players slept upstairs at the fine hotel, while the gamblers hassled over odds and placed their bets in the lobby.

Even before the first game on October 1, the *Boston Post* wrote that "thousands of dollars are being wagered on the result of the series between the two teams." Serious gambling began two days before the first pitch at Boston's Huntington Avenue Grounds:

> The biggest single bet was made during the afternoon [of September 29] when Sport Sullivan bet $3500 that Boston wins the series. Frank M. Question of the Pittsburgh Dispatch, acting for a Pittsburgh supporter, telegraphed $2000 to cover Sullivan's money. Another big bet was between two brokers doing business in the Frasier building, $500 being bet on the Collins team [Boston] against $450. The remaining bets yesterday were mostly small and Boston was the ruling favorite at 5 to 4.
>
> Tomorrow a large party of Pittsburgh sports is expected to reach here and it is reported that they are loaded with money to back the Pirates. They will find it an easy matter to place their bets. Boston will be the favorite and the odds of yesterday are expected to remain stationary until the first game, at least, has been played.

The *Post* said that a total $50,000 was expected to be wagered on the entire series, but it would total much more in the end: "One bet made in a downtown resort [a gambling parlor] which occasioned much comment was one of $100 against $1000 that Boston fails to win a game. Both parties wanted their names kept secret."

By September 30, the betting had become frenzied. The highest individual wager that night was $2,500, made by Fred J. Marshall of Boston's Hotel Langham. After a three-hour period of wager making, betting seemed to slow, although "Big Bill" Kelliher, a well known former college football player, wagered a $75 suit of clothes that Boston would prevail in the series.

Boston was the clear betting favorite for the first game at 10 to 7 with Cy Young set to take the mound for the hometown nine. On the afternoon of October 1 before the first pitch was thrown, over $10,000 had been wagered on the game. Sport Sullivan, a fixture on Boston's gambling scene for many years, covered the largest portion of the action. The newspapers reported that he quickly snapped up any money that Pittsburgh supporters wanted to gamble. Sullivan would be a key figure 16 years later in fixing the 1919 series.

Betting proceeded in the grandstand throughout the first game, "although here the betting was carried on in a more quiet manner, and was mostly of the friendly character, $5 and $10 wagers being the rule." The first game was a disaster on the field for the Boston nine. The Pirates scored four runs in the top of the first inning and the Boston club never caught up. Yet the defeat did not scare away Boston's gamblers. A cartoon on the front page of the *Boston Herald* the next day pictured an elderly Pittsburgh rooter driving away with his wagon filled with cash, but the Boston rooter, with barrels of money, was still game: "Never mind old man," he says, "You'll need all of that before we're through with you!"

The *Herald* predicted the odds would shift closer to even money for game two, but Pittsburgh bettors demanded a greater advantage. $25,000 was bet, again with Sport Sullivan as the major player. No one would take bets on the outcome of the entire series until they saw how Boston's second hurler Bill Dinneen fared against the Pittsburgh "Champions of the West." The Pittsburgh delegation was right to hold on to their money. Dineen whipped the Pirates with a three-hit shutout to even the series. Betting on game three before an overflow crowd remained remarkably light. Every time Boston stalwart Buck Freeman came to bat, however, bets flew on whether he would hit safely. (He never did.) "The local sports are a pretty sore lot," the *Boston Herald* reported.

All the Boston papers carried rumors that the local nine had thrown a game to make sure the series would extend beyond five or six games. "Men who took the two defeats most bitterly to heart have not hesitated in saying that at least one of these three games was 'not on the level,' that Boston could have won the series had it chosen." The *Boston Post* offered this rebuttal:

> Those who have followed the game of baseball for years past are scoffing at these stories, however. They claim that they are all simply fictions from the dizzy brains of Boston gamblers, who have bet "not wisely but too well." These people state that any attempt on the part of either team to deliberately "throw" a game would be at once apparent to the keen-eyed spectator; that such a proceeding would ring the death knell of baseball as a professional sport.

The *Herald* quoted the treasurer of Boston's National League club, J. B. Billingsley, as its expert on game fixing. He opined that he thought "all three games were remarkably sharp and clean. The team that played the best ball won each day." Billingsley then waxed eloquently:

> The thing that makes baseball national is its cleanliness — its honesty. Any attempt at crookedness would mean immediate exposure and the end of the offender's career. Besides, the baseball public could easily detect it. Baseball is a clean, honest, manly sport. Crookedness simply cannot enter into it.

That night, 125 Boston gamblers traveled west on the same private train as the ball club to take up the series in Pittsburgh the following week. Boston's Royal Rooters, including many notorious sports, brought their money with them to support their heroes in the betting pools. And the Boston newspapers — there were ten dailies at the time — would dutifully report the betting news from "the West" together with descriptions of the contests.

Betting in Pittsburgh, according to the *Boston Post*, was slow "although the roll brought from Boston to back [Jimmy] Collins' team at reasonable odds is big enough to burn a 'wet elephant.'" The *Herald* assured its readers that the Boston rooters "have plenty of money with them and are ready to put it out on the boys. But they do not propose to throw it away as they did in the games in Boston." Now with the Pirates ahead in the series two games to one with four games scheduled for their home Exposition Park along the Alleghany River, it was the Boston gamblers who demanded odds. No wagers were forthcoming, however. During the fourth game, the money would not flow. In the top half of the fifth inning of that game, the Americans rallied to tie the score and Charlie Lavis, a leader of the Boston faithful,

> with a megaphone in hand offered to bet any man in the grandstand $100 to $30 that Pittsburgh would not score again during the game. He could not get a man to take up his proposition and he immediately offered $100 to $50 that Boston would score again before the end of the game, but there were no takers.

"Talk about the pikers," Boston rooter Jack Keenan told the *Post*, "I haven't even taken the rubber band off my roll!"

The Pirates won game four and now led the series three games to one. Pittsburgh's captain Fred Clarke selected William "Brickyard" Kennedy, a controversial choice as a senior hurler, to pitch game five. The portents seemed to favor Kennedy, however. He hailed from Bellaire, Ohio, only sixty miles to the west of Pittsburgh, and many of his hometown friends traveled to Pittsburgh to watch him pitch. It was also Kennedy's thirty-sixth birthday. He reported that he was eager to "twirl," and he told the newspapers that he placed a wager that he would win his game. He didn't. It was a sad birthday for Kennedy, and it would be his last appearance in the major leagues after a twelve-year career.

Sam Leever would take the mound for Pittsburgh the next day for game six, and Pirates' fanatics were heartened when the newspapers reported that he had wagered $300 "of his own money at even [odds] that he would win." Betting picked up at Newell's Café, a local betting establishment. "Pittsburgh money at even odds was snapped up eagerly," the *Boston Post* reported, characterizing the gambling as "lively." The Boston club triumphed again, however, having reversed their slide. The series was now tied at three games for each club, but the Pirates had one more opportunity to win a game at home.

The Pirates' ace hurler Deacon Phillippe would pitch game seven for the club, and for once the odds favored the Pirates. In the series so far, Phillippe had bested the Bostons twice in the Hub and once again in game four. Betting was at even odds, or even favored the Pirates, as their ace started his fourth series game. The Boston batters had finally learned his tricks, however.

Over $10,000 was wagered on the game, according to the *Herald:* "Every cent the Pittsburgh men offered was grabbed by the Boston rooters." Their allegiance proved profitable as Boston prevailed, "and a happier trainload of men than pulled out of here at 7 o'clock tonight would be hard to imagine," as Boston headed home leading the series four games to three.

The eighth and final game back at the Huntington Avenue Grounds in Boston produced little gambling action. It seemed the Pittsburgh faithful no longer had their hearts (or their money) in the game. The Pittsburgh owner, Barney Dreyfuss, who had first conceived of a world series and proposed it as a challenge match, had put up a heavy wager on his club to prevail. According to the *Post*, he was "desperate to win." However, his club would not be able to touch Boston hurler Bill Dineen even for one run.

Boston's gamblers cashed in on their bets. Sport Sullivan reported to the *Post* that he won $4,000. Charlie Lavis netted $2,500 and Charley Waldron $1,500. Big Bill Kelliher won his $75 suit of clothes. "More than 500 hats were probably won on the series and several freak bets will furnish some amusement when carried out," reported the *Post*. Regretfully, the newspaper did not report on the nature of the "freak bets."

The Odds Against Enforcement

Although organized baseball continued to preach against gambling, it continued unabated. Both the fans and the participants in the game put money on the line. The great manager John McGraw openly placed a $400 wager on his National League Champion Giants to defeat the American League Athletics in the 1905 World Series. (At the same time, newspapers claimed that New York gamblers had bribed the Athletics' left-handed star pitcher Rube Waddell who suddenly took ill and could not play.) The Giants prevailed in five games nonetheless, and McGraw collected his winnings without suffering any disciplinary repercussions.

Many clubs sought to deter gambling by posting signs inside the ballpark: "NO BETTING ALLOWED IN THIS PARK." Like most other efforts before Judge Landis took over as commissioner of the game, these notices did little to deter the practice. For a time, clubs would not announce their starting pitchers until game time, making the setting of odds away from the park on game day more difficult. These efforts may have been well-intentioned, but they proved futile.

Occasionally, ball clubs would call upon the local constabulary to stop open gambling at the ball parks. In Philadelphia on June 20, 1907, the police raided Columbia Park, the home field of the Athletics, and "captured four notorious offenders." The club had hoped to arrest at least a hundred gamblers, but, according to the *Washington Post*, apparently "this was their off day." Later it was revealed that an employee of the club had tipped off the gambling regulars about the coming raid.

Baseball's efforts to control gambling on the outcome of games by fans and players alike ran into the reality that odds-playing was an accepted part of American life. Governments winked at these non-violent violations of the law. In such a context, it was difficult for public officials to muster moral outrage against betting on baseball. Hypocrisy was an unsteady guard against wrongdoing.

Periodically, organized baseball and the press boldly tried to hide the connection between gambling and the sport. In a masterful piece of self-deception in 1904 published in the *Washington Post*, Philadelphia owner and manager Connie Mack boasted that the game had rooted out all gambling and game fixing. The prevailing rule was banishment from the game for those who would gamble: "It was the strict enforcement of this rule which made professional baseball the most honest field sport in vogue." The *Post* reassured its readers three years later:

> Professional baseball is an honest sport nowadays. It was purged of any crookedness long ago, and, whatever else its faults, is on the level and appeals to reputable, intelligent people.

Despite these protestations, gambling continued apace. American League President Ban Johnson in 1908 called upon clubs to take stern measures to stamp out gambling even if that required "arresting every one caught at the parks making bets." On August 4, 1908, the City of Boston disapproved the renewal of Boston National League club's license because of concerns about gambling at its South End grounds. Apparently, the American League Red Sox club had done a better job patrolling its field, the adjacent Huntington Avenue Grounds, against gambling.

Gambling continued to haunt the national game. In 1911, Garry Herrmann, the owner of the Cincinnati club who was chairman of baseball's national commission, announced that from then on telegraph companies would refuse to deliver telegrams that facilitated nationwide gambling. In 1912, the president of the Philadelphia Athletics swore out warrants that led to the arrest of 25 men at his ballpark for gambling. Other clubs escorted their gamblers from the grounds, and periodically baseball officials publicly rued the connection between their sport and gambling.

As the decade of the 1910s drew to a close, open gambling on baseball reached its peak. With the race tracks closed during the First World War, gamblers turned to the national game as the subject of their wagers. Most baseball fans were content with an occasional wager on a game, but spectators were not above interrupting a game that, if it were completed, would result in substantial betting loses.

A contest on June 16, 1917, between the Chicago White Sox and the Boston Red Sox had to be cancelled because hundreds of Boston's gambling spectators rushed on to the field at Fenway Park before the third out was made in the home fifth inning. The timing was purposeful. As an unofficial game, no losing bets would need to be paid. The *Chicago Tribune* reported that Umpire McCormick called time and the melee ensued: "On the whole, it was the boldest piece of business ever perpetrated by a baseball crowd." Odds-makers in the right field pavilion, who had been "allowed to operate freely," had instigated the incident.

Serious gamblers were prepared to use all available means to weigh the odds in their favor. They would use the press to inflate the odds based on false information. In 1920, for example, gamblers fed the newspapers a false report about a car wreck injury to the Yankees new star, Babe Ruth. Ruth was fine, but the odds favoring the Yankees' opponent, the Cleveland Indians, spiked, providing a huge payoff for Gotham's gamblers.

Gambling and Baseball Today

In the last sixty years, the commissioner's office has only addressed gambling's connection to the game intermittently. In 1947, commissioner Happy Chandler suspended Dodger manager Leo Durocher for a season based on his "social" relationships with gangsters Bugsy Siegel and Joe Adonis. The concern, of course, was the potential influence of gambling on baseball. Commissioner Bowie Kuhn was the most doctrinaire on the issue. He fined Clete Boyer $1,000 for betting on college and professional football games in 1968 and 1969. In 1970 Kuhn suspended Detroit pitcher Denny McLain, the Cy Young winner the two previous seasons, for his involvement with bookmakers, who allegedly had crippled him during the season for not paying his debts. It was not McLain's first encounter with the mob. In September 1967, mobster Tony Giacolone stomped on McLain's foot, dislocating two toes, because the pitcher had failed to make timely payments.

Commissioner Kuhn also used his powers to keep owners and managers away from troubling outside influences. He ordered club owners Charles Finley and Bill Bartholomay to divest themselves of holdings in companies that owned casinos. He barred Baltimore manager Joe Altobelli and Cleveland skipper Mike Ferraro from participating in race track promotions. Commissioner Fay Vincent suspended two umpires, Frank Pulli and Rich Garcia, for gambling.

In the last six decades, only three men associated with baseball have been barred from the game for life because of gambling-related offenses. On October 29, 1979, Commissioner Kuhn banned Willie Mays, one of the game's all-time greats, because he had signed a contract with Bally's Resorts in Atlantic City as a public relations executive. The banishment occurred a few months after Mays was inducted into the Hall of Fame. On February 8, 1983, Kuhn punished Mickey Mantle for his association with gambling interests in Atlantic City. Although warned by Kuhn, Mantle accepted a job at the Claridge Resort and Casino for $100,000 a year as director of sports promotions planning golf tournaments. Kuhn explained to the press: "I have told Mickey Mantle I have no choice...." When Peter Ueberroth replaced Kuhn as commissioner in 1985, he immediately reinstated the two great stars who had long abandoned their positions with the Atlantic City interests. The third, and most infamous, case of banishment was Pete Rose, whose case we will address in the concluding chapter.

Some clubs, on occasion, tried to stem gambling at their ball parks. The New York Yankees hired special agents who would mingle with the crowd looking for gamblers. Gatekeepers would keep known gamblers out and post their pictures in the box offices. Periodically, the newspapers would report arrests for wagering. In 1940, for example, the *New York Times* reported that three men were arrested at Philadelphia's Shibe Park and fined $12.50 each for "disorderly conduct" related to gambling, hardly a significant deterrent to the practice.

Conclusion

Gambling in modern America has lost all semblance of deviance from the social norm. Promoted by the corporate culture and state governments, all moral outrage against gambling seems to have disappeared. Despite America's current religious revival, no one seems to worry whether gambling is immoral. The Catholic Church discovered bingo as a needed source of revenue. Indian tribes have brought casino gambling opportunities to within easy reach of most urban populations. Governments have reaped enormous tax receipts from sanctioned gambling and multiplying lottery jackpots. Las Vegas flowered in the desert based on the attraction of legalized gambling, and it became America's prime vacation destination. Respectability quickly followed suit.

With the explosion of modern computer technology, gambling has become totally divorced from place or time. On-line betting is a multi-billion dollar business beyond the reach of easy regulation. Sports betting is the fastest growing segment of the sports business, and its practice no longer provides headlines in our daily papers.

Baseball has in some ways accepted the new reality. By 1998, clubs were allowed to accept advertising money from casinos. Commissioner Bud Selig explained: "After all, gambling is legal everywhere. So as life changes and society changes, frankly, we also have made some changes." Selig had no comment when it was reported in 1997 that Albert Belle lost $40,000 gambling in sports other than baseball. It seems that now the commissioner's office only proscribes illegal gambling. There are risks, nonetheless. Commissioner Fay Vincent explained in The *Sporting News* in 1991: "A fix is virtually inconceivable." That, he acknowledged, is what people might have said before 1919 as well.

Henry Chadwick fully understood the risk 150 years ago. The association between gambling and baseball ultimately served to undermine the sport. All the ever-delighting qualities of the game — the challenge between the pitcher and the batter, the splendid play afield that stems a rally, the towering drive over the outer boundary wall — are irrelevant to the gambler. He sees only the outcome of each pitch, each at bat, each inning in the contest as important. Whether the result is the product of splendid athleticism or mindless carelessness matters not. The bet is won or lost not based on the quality of the performance, but the outcome. When it is only gambling that matters, we lose the essence of the national game.

Judge Landis's calculated response to the acquittal of the Black Sox and
his autocratic rule over the major leagues for the next quarter century would
renew the public's confidence in baseball and save the game.

Chapter 3
Game Fixing

Regardless of the verdict of juries, no player that throws a ball game, no player that entertains proposals or promises to throw a game, no player that sits in a conference with a bunch of crooked players and gamblers where the ways and means of throwing games are discussed, and does not promptly tell his club about it, will ever again play professional baseball. — Commissioner Kenesaw Mountain Landis

ON SEPTEMBER 27, 1920, only days before the scheduled beginning of the 1920 World Series, Jimmy Isaminger of the *Philadelphia North-American* reported that the 1919 World Series had been fixed. Billy Maharg, one of the gambler-conspirators, had confessed and spilled the story to his hometown newspaper. Maharg had various sports connections. He boxed in Philadelphia, played one major league game with Detroit in 1912 and another with the Phillies in 1916. He owned a few race horses and had been Pete Alexander's chauffeur for a while. His conversation with Isaminger, however, turned the world of sports upside-down. With the fix exposed, there was little betting on the Cleveland-Brooklyn match-up set to begin the following week at Ebbets Field. Just to be safe, Indians manager Tris Speaker kept the identity of his starting pitcher, Stan Coveleski, secret until game time.

Not coincidentally, less than two months later, on November 12, 1920, the magnates of the game appointed Federal Judge Kenesaw Mountain Landis as Organized Baseball's first commissioner. Baseball's premier game-fixing scandal would scar the national pastime, but Judge Landis's calculated response to the acquittal of the Black Sox and his autocratic rule over the major leagues for the next quarter century would renew the public's confidence in baseball and save the game. The events of 1919, however, were not unique in the history of baseball. In fact, they were the continuation of more than a half century of chicanery. Baseball had long been infected with "the fix."

Baseball's game-fixing catastrophe of 1919 mirrored the contemporary national experience. A few weeks after the press broke the story of the 1919 World Series, American voters (including, for the first time, women voters) elected Warren G. Harding as their 29th president. Certainly among our least able national leaders, Harding would preside over a thoroughly corrupt regime. Harding brought his "Ohio Gang" to Washington. They looted the national treasury, as Harding played golf and poker and regularly attended Washington Senators baseball games at Griffiths Stadium. His Secretary of the Interior Albert B. Fall and Secretary of the Navy Edwin C. Denby were among the most notable miscreants of the Republican clique. In exchange for bribes, Fall sold the drilling rights under the Teapot Dome Indian Reservation that Denby had urged Harding to transfer from Navy control. Other Harding officeholders skimmed profits, demanded kickbacks and even ran alcohol and drug rings. Fraud and bribery were a way of life in official Washington, even more than they were in baseball.

Baseball's crisis exemplified the decline in American morals in the period following the First World War. Private sector entrepreneurs across the country, freed from governmental oversight, were full participants in the blazing avarice of the Roaring Twenties. President Coolidge, who succeeded to the presidency upon Harding's death, restated the prevailing ethos: "The business of America is business. Business is one of the greatest contributing forces to the moral and spiritual advancement of the race."

New businesses thrived. For almost a century, religious and social leaders had worked tirelessly to ban the sale of alcohol. Prohibition, their great success, created a new thriving and illegal sector of the economy built on bootleg alcohol. At the same time, respectable businessmen took advantage of the laissez-faire regulation of commerce to extend monopoly control over supplies, territories, and prices and systematically extract excess profits from the marketplace. And baseball flourished as never before.

It was a golden age of all forms of American enterprise — team sports, entrepreneurship, crime and plunder. Americans celebrated with abandon, freed from wartime constraints and astonished by rapidly developing technologies. The victims of the age — the urban and rural poor, small businesses, and the children of former slaves — all remained invisible to a public more interested in the exploits of gangsters such as John Dillinger. Babe Ruth was a man for all America. He strode mightily on the national stage, a symbol of true excess, who played America's game better than anyone had ever played it before.

The Commissioner

The establishment of the powerful office of "high commissioner" of baseball was the culmination of a series of events played out over many years in the baseball business. Although nominally just the President of the American League, Ban Johnson had exercised uncontested authority well beyond his official portfolio as organized baseball's de facto overseer for almost two decades. His use and abuse of power created enemies among the sixteen club owners, each used to absolute power in his own realm. Johnson, much taken with his own importance to the game, exercised authority in an arbitrary fashion. He held petty grudges, much like the club owners themselves. As the decade of 1910s drew to a close, his supremacy was coming to an end.

There were a series of high profile cases that heightened owner animosity towards Johnson. Under Johnson's leadership, the National Commission's decisions were final and binding, much in the same way as umpires enforced the rules of baseball on the field. Losers often went away sore and sometimes they went to court despite their promise in the National Agreement that they would not. In 1915, the National Commission declared future Hall of Famer George Sisler a free agent, although he had signed a contract with Pirates owner Barney Dreyfuss. Dreyfuss, once a Johnson loyalist, became a Johnson adversary. After the 1918 season, the National Commission upheld the technical claim of the Boston Braves to pitcher Scott Perry, but Athletics owner Connie Mack sued to keep his promising right hander. Mack ultimately kept his pitcher, who had won twenty games in 1918, but won only 18 games over the remaining three years of his major league career. The matter was settled with a financial payment to Boston, but hard feelings remained. In 1920, Johnson vetoed the Red Sox sale of Carl Mays to the Yankees for $40,000 and some minor players. The Yankees obtained an injunction in a New York court against Johnson, and in open court referred to him as an "unmolested despot." The case was heard by then Judge, later Senator, Robert Wagner of New York; he sided with the home town Yankee club.

Ban Johnson's generation-long tenure, his waning ability to resolve disputes effectively, and the growing concern among the club magnates about the impact of the gambling cancer on baseball eventually led the owners to consider various plans to reform or replace the National Commission. Albert D. Lasker, a Chicago advertising man and an important minority stockholder of the Cubs, suggested that the game turn to non-baseball men to administer its business. After all, with a few notable exceptions such as Connie Mack and Charles Comiskey, the owners themselves did not have major league playing experience before purchasing their franchises. Lasker proposed maintaining the three-man board, but employing a well-paid non-baseball chairman to run the show.

Lasker certainly knew how to sell a product to the public. After masterminding the advertising campaign for Van Camp Pork and Beans, Sunkist orange juice and Lucky Strikes cigarettes, in 1918 Lasker and his Chicago firm, Lord & Thomas, took on the challenge of defeating the League of Nations for the Republican Party. Two years later he packaged Warren G. Harding for the American voting public using advertising techniques.

Building on Lasker's proposal, the club owners vetted a series of potential candidates for the chairman's position, including former president William Howard Taft, war heroes General George Pershing and General Leonard Wood, Senator Hiram Johnson, and ex-treasury secretary William McAdoo. National League president John Heydler set forth the particulars of their search:

> We want a man as chairman who will rule with an iron hand. I'll
> be glad to take orders if I am told something is wrong at a certain

place and instructed to clean it up. Baseball has lacked a hand of that type for years. It needs it now worse than ever. Therefore, it is our object to appoint a big man to lead the new commission.

Finally, the leaders of the game settled on federal judge Kenesaw Mountain Landis to become the singular head of the game.

Landis accepted the position with significant conditions. He would be paid $50,000 a year, more than five times his salary as a federal judge, but he would also keep his lifetime position as a federal judge. (Landis resigned his judicial post a year into his commissioner's term when several congressmen threatened to impeach him.) Landis would not be the chairman of a three-person board, but rather serve as the one-man ruler of baseball. To make sure the terms were clear, Landis drafted his own charter as the "First High Commissioner" of the enterprise he would rule for a quarter century. It provided for "unreviewable control [of] all ethical matters."

At first, Landis would appear to have been an unconventional choice for the magnates. He had no experience in the game other than playing on the dirt ball fields of Logansport, Indiana, as a youngster and attending numerous professional games during each season in Chicago. Appointed to the federal bench by Theodore Roosevelt, Landis had established a reputation as a fearless trust-busting judge who knew how to command the public spotlight. He once summoned John D. Rockefeller from New York to appear in his Chicago courtroom and fined Standard Oil almost thirty million dollars.

Landis had auditioned for the baseball job a few years earlier when the owners of the rival Federal League filed an antitrust action against the Major League owners in his federal court, thinking that Landis, the trust buster, would be a favorable choice. They had misjudged the Judge, who boldly stated "any blows at the thing called baseball would be regarded by this court as a blow to a national institution." Landis stalled the litigation in its tracks. After its second and last season, the Federal Leaguers settled with Organized Baseball, and Landis apparently had passed his audition.

In many ways, Landis was the perfect choice to become the king of the baseball kingdom. Landis was a self-made man who had dropped out of high school, like most of the magnates. He tried to work as a railroad brakeman, a bicycle racer, and a roller skating rink operator, but finally found employment as a journalist, before finishing night law school and practicing law. As a judge, Landis was an autocrat who would countenance no criticism from anyone. He was an opinionated absolutist who had followed his own version of the law on the bench even in the face of almost certain reversal on appeal. As commissioner, he would not suffer review again, because there would be no appeal from his decisions.

Landis brought to the game a total confidence in the righteousness and morality of his personal vision and a full appreciation of his boundless and unreviewable authority. The *Chicago Tribune* reported that an eight-man delegation of club owners entered his courtroom "hats in hand" to anoint him while the judge was trying an income-tax bribery case. Landis "sharply banged his gavel down and told them to make less noise." He had them escorted to his chambers where he kept them waiting for 45 minutes. Finally, he accepted their offer, he said, in order "to keep the crooks out of baseball."

The sixteen major league clubs entered into a Memorandum of Agreement with Judge Landis on January 12, 1921. They agreed to submit themselves to the jurisdiction of the "party of the second part," that is, Landis. Landis, in turn, accepted his "election" as commissioner, noting to the press that this new position would allow him to render "additional public service."

As Ed Fitzgerald wrote in *Sport Magazine* after Landis's death: "The Judge was the kind of man who could strut sitting down." Often found at Chicago baseball games during his reign — "his old black slouch hat pulled down over his eyes and a long black cape falling from his shoulder"— Landis gladly shouldered the burdens of sovereignty. Landis explained to the press that he took the position of supreme ruler so that the little kids would always have their game of baseball.

Commissioner Landis quickly staked out his position on the pending

Chicago Black Sox scandal: "The only thing in anyone's mind now," Landis said, "is to make and keep baseball what the millions of fans throughout the United States want it to be." He signaled his intention to punish any wrongdoers: "If I catch any crook in baseball, the rest of his life is going to be a hot one."

Landis kept his promise. After deliberating less than three hours on the evening of August 2, 1921, the criminal jury acquitted eight Chicago American League ballplayers of all criminal charges. The courtroom, according to the *Tribune*, turned into "a love feast as the jurors, lawyers and defendants clapped each other on the back and exchanged congratulations." The jurors "grinned like schoolboys." Landis then banned the players from the game of baseball for life "regardless of the verdict of juries." The *Tribune* regaled his action as giving the game a much needed "character bath." Landis assured the public: "There is absolutely no chance for any of them to creep back into organized baseball. They will be and remain outlaws."

Although his action may have been arbitrary, Landis' purgative was a critical step in redeeming the integrity of the game in the public's mind. It was also exactly what the magnates wanted and needed him to do. Even Charles Comiskey, who lost thousands of dollars in contract value when eight of his White Sox star players were banned from the game, applauded Landis' action. During his quarter-century reign as commissioner, Landis would forgive the transgressions of some famous players, like Cobb and Speaker — "These players have not been, nor are they now, found guilty of fixing a ball game"— and punish some lesser lights with astonishing severity. In retrospect, however, his banishment of the Black Sox was necessary and proper, even if it was harsh. In the public's mind, Landis cleansed baseball of game fixing.

The gambling culture had long been part of the national game. For decades, baseball players had openly wagered on the outcome of contests in which they played. The Black Sox caper, however, made public the venal sin of fixing games. A seemingly innocent bet on the outcome of a game was one thing; a deliberate effort to alter the outcome of that game or a series of games by not playing up to one's best — by "laying down"— was certainly another. It raised the most serious risk to the legitimacy and integrity of the game that baseball ever faced.

Landis stood steadfast:

> Baseball is something more than a game to an American boy. It is his training field for life work. Destroy his faith in its squareness and honesty, and you have destroyed something more; you have planted suspicion of all things in his heart.

A History of Chicanery

Baseball as we know it today had its genesis on a cricket pitch on the heights above Hoboken, New Jersey in the mid-1840s. The rules for the contests were drafted by a member of the Knickerbocker social and athletic club, surveyor Alexander Cartwright, in September 1845, and young Manhattan athletes ferried across the Hudson to play this new version of a bat-and-ball game during the spring of 1846. Nothing in Cartwright's Knickerbocker rules prohibited betting or throwing contests. After all, this was a game for persons of high moral character who would enjoy the athletic competition after work. Who would even think of rigging the outcome? Why would anyone want to do such a thing?

The historical record shows that for most of the nineteenth century and for the first two decades of the twentieth century, people did want to do such a thing. Baseball was infested with corruption. Unscrupulous players allied with gambling interests regularly fixed contests. The greatest promoter of the sport, Albert Spalding, admitted that "sold games" were a common thing. On occasion, the seamy practice of hippodroming was exposed to public light, but we can never know for sure how many matches had predetermined outcomes. At the same time as this vice grew, baseball became one of America's favorite activities for both participants and spectators.

To be considered a national game, of course, would require the sport to have structure and organization. In March 1857, at a meeting in a New York City hotel, fourteen baseball clubs from the metropolitan area organized themselves into the amateur National Association of Base Ball Players. The Association's charter expressly prohibited both professionalism and betting by its members. It was the first recognition of the corrupting influence of money and gambling on the purely amateur enterprise.

At the same time that baseball began achieving national recognition, America's entrepreneurs were cashing in on the wealth of the continent. With drive and determination, but little concern for legal proprieties, in a single generation in a Gilded Age of excess, a cadre of American businessmen parlayed financial schemes into enormous untaxed profits and created an aristocracy of wealth. The tycoons first made immense fortunes from Civil War profiteering. They then played the game of unregulated economics with the same vigor as ballplayers played the game of baseball. Until the progressives finally enacted legislation and courts began enforcing the law, the robber barons ruled the American economy.

When the terrible slaughter and destruction of the Civil War had ended, the businesses that had stoked the engines of the Northern victory over the slave-owning agrarian aristocracy of the South were transformed into national financial machines. Those who had survived the military catastrophe were emboldened to profit by any means possible. It is no surprise that this impulse motivated baseball players as well. The sportsmanship that had characterized the early game gave way to personal morality and the profit motive.

The first recorded instance of players throwing a contest for pay occurred shortly after the close of the Civil War. On September 28, 1865, the much-favored New York Mutuals team squared off against their arch rivals, the Brooklyn Eckfords, in a contest held in the Elysian Fields grounds in Hoboken. Some four thousand spectators came to view the contest. The Eckfords' Frank Pidgeon summed up the feeling of many about the wonderful new national game:

> We would forget business and everything else on Tuesday afternoons, go out into the green fields, don our ball suits, and go at

it with a perfect rush. At such times, we were boys again. Such sport as this brightens a man up and improves him both in mind and body.

The game began as expected with the Mutuals ahead 5–4 after the first four innings. Then the Mutuals' catcher William Wansley began to systematically fail to catch anything behind the plate. The Eckfords scored eleven runs in the fifth inning, many on passed balls. The *New York Times* reported: "Overpitched balls, wild throws, passed balls and failures to stop them in the field marked the play of the Mutuals to an unusual extent." The Mutuals team captain moved Wansley to right field, but the club could never catch up. The Eckfords trounced the Mutuals 23–11. The *New York Clipper* reported that there was some "talk" about the players "selling the game," although it hoped the talk was not true.

Concerned about their club's performance that day, the Mutuals charged catcher Wansley with "willful and designed inattention" in his play. An investigation revealed that the night before the contest gambler Kane McLoughlin had paid Wansley one hundred dollars to make sure that the Eckfords would prevail. Wansley, in turn, approached third baseman Ed Duffy who agreed to join the conspiracy as long as shortstop Thomas Devyr was part of the plot.

The two infielders, Duffy and Devyr, each pocketed $30 and Wansley had $40 as a payoff for "laying down." Gambler McLoughlin collected on the bets he had placed on the Brooklyn club. When the scandal was revealed, the players claimed they themselves had been the victims of a "wicked conspiracy." Later, Devyr explained that Wansley told him:

> We can lose this game without doing the Club any harm, and win the home-and-home game.... Now you ain't got a cent, nor neither has Duffy; you can make this money without any one being a bit the wiser of it.

Finally, Wansley made a full confession about the scheme. The annual convention of the National Association of Base Ball Players declared the thrown game to be "null and void" and banned two of the miscreants — Wansley and Duffy — from baseball. Because the Mutuals needed Devyr and because he was said to be but a lad of 18 (he was likely much older), the Association excused the shortstop from further punishment after missing the 1866 season. In any case, by 1870 the Mutuals would return Wansley and Duffy to the club with the Association's approval.

It is not surprising that the New York Mutuals would lead off the history of baseball's game-fixing scandals. The president of the baseball club was William March "Boss" Tweed, the infamous leader of New York's Tammany Hall. The Mutuals were formed from Tweed's volunteer fire company, a source of significant political power in Manhattan in the 1860s. Tweed put all his amateur Mutuals players on the City's patronage payroll in "Clerkships in Tax Offices, Inspectorships of Streets, Sewers, Docks and other city places"— Tweed was by then the deputy streets commissioner and controlled over 500 patronage jobs — although it is unlikely any of the ballplayers ever attended to their assigned jobs. (Of course, this was common practice among many "amateur" clubs. The players on the Washington Nationals, for example, all held no-work federal government jobs.) Tweed also put the officers of the Mutuals club on the employment rolls of the coroner's office. John Wildey, a leader of the baseball club, was the city coroner and a Tammany Hall official.

Boss Tweed was a master of corruption, although there is no evidence he participated in the comparatively minor Wansley set up. During the reign of the Tweed Ring, hundreds of millions of dollars were swindled from New York City and its private contractors. Tweed controlled the City's bureaucracy, and, as a result, manipulated its finances. Tweed's municipal thievery included simple graft and the solicitation of bribes and kickbacks from all who wanted to do business with the booming municipality. A standard fifteen percent was included in all municipal contracts to pay the Tweed Ring. At the height of his tenure, Tweed was the third largest landowner in the City and extended his personal influence over railroads, banks and hotels. He is said to have skimmed 45 million dollars from the treasury, equal to the annual federal budget.

Boss Tweed's reign, however, came to an end in late 1871. In July of that year, the *New York Times* published detailed evidence of his illegal operation. Thomas Nast did much to turn public opinion against the Boss with his biting cartoons in *Harper's Weekly*. Tweed is said to have cried: "Stop them damned pictures. I don't care so much what the papers say about me. My constituents can't read. But, damn it, they can see pictures!" He was arrested and tried for, among other things, "failure to audit claims against the city." After one hung jury trial, Tweed was convicted and eventually died in prison.

The Organization of the Game

After the Civil War, the number of baseball clubs in the National Association grew exponentially, to 91 by 1865, to 202 in 1866, and to more than 300 by 1867. Within that short period of time, the game had taken on an unsavory aspect. There was much justified suspicion that the games were for sale. In 1867, *Harper's Weekly* referred to the "tricks by which games have been 'sold' for the benefit of gamblers." Although baseball had established itself as a "godsend to American youth," according to *The Galaxy* magazine in October 1868, "professional gamblers are putting [the game's] popularity in jeopardy. Such havoc have these gentry made of late that hardly a great match comes off without suspicions of foul play. Base-ball is infested by blacklegs." From the earliest days of its organization, the sport risked falling into total disrepute.

The National Association elected George Sands as its president in 1868, expressing the hope that his ascendancy would stem gambling, professionalism and game fixing. Sands had plainly stated his opposition to the gambling "infection" and, as *Harper's Weekly* reported, he sought the support of the "moral and educated classes of the community." Yet, gambling and game-fixing stories commanded the public's attention, and, as a result, attendance at games dropped precipitously. Contests that had regularly drawn 15,000 spectators in 1867 would only attract 5,000 attendees two years later.

At the same time that the scandals surfaced, organized baseball transformed itself from an organization of amateur teams run by the players themselves into a collection of clubs of professional athletes under the direction of non-playing management. Baseball, like most of America in the post-war era, had become a business.

In 1869, the Cincinnati Red Stockings, the first openly-professional club, toured the nation playing all comers without suffering a loss. Upon returning to the Queen City, the City Fathers feted their ballplayers and presented them with a "champion bat," twenty-seven feet long and nine inches in diameter. Providing a salary for these baseball professionals — the total team payroll was $9,000 — was designed to make them less vulnerable to entreaties from gamblers. Of course, long before the Cincinnati businessmen founded their traveling road show (the club played no home games on the banks of the Ohio) "amateur" sides had hired "ringers" and paid them with no-work jobs or under-the-table cash. One such hired hand was Albert Spalding, who would become the most important leader of the baseball business in the nineteenth century. In his 1911 memoirs, *America's National Game*, Spalding justified the professionalism model as the only way to defeat "the gambling element":

[The gamblers] had so long been a controlling influence that anything threatening their ascendancy was sure to meet with stubborn resistance. Of course, their chief interest in Base Ball was what they could make out of it in the line of their nefarious profession. They feared that if the executive control of the game passed into the hands of men who also had cash at stake, it was a sure thing that just in so far as the management made money they must lose. They knew, of course, that the clubs must depend upon gate receipts for their income; that gate receipts depended upon the restoration of public confidence, and that public confidence could only be won back by the eradication of the gambling evil.

Under Spalding's prevailing philosophy, only businessmen could keep the game clean by claiming the profits created by the players' performances. As we shall see, Spalding's self-serving encomium proved a shallow prophecy. It would be very difficult to keep the game clean under any organizational structure.

The National Association staggered to its demise in the 1870 season. Bill Craver, a "sure and reliable" catcher with the Chicago White Stockings, according to reporter Henry Chadwick, was expelled from his club on August 18, 1870, based on allegations of "receiving money for not winning games." Craver denied the charges, but his expulsion was confirmed at the convention of the National Association. He would resume his baseball career, however, the following season with the Troy Haymakers, a member of a new professional league. Craver would return to the annals of hippodroming ballplayers six years later when he played for the infamous 1877 Louisville Grays and participated in the greatest baseball fixing scandal of the nineteenth century.

Although proof of actual game fixing was rare, the specter encouraged many to believe that all contests were rigged. The *Brooklyn Spirit* reported in 1870 that interest in the hometown Atlantics' games had dropped because the club was "getting into such bad repute, from the constantly flying rumors of 'sells' and 'thrown' games, that few people care to expend their time and money in going to witness what may turn out to be merely a 'hippodroming' exhibition."

Despite its best efforts at purification during a time of explosive growth, the National Association could not shake the public's perception of a connection between gambling and the game. On March 16, 1871, according to the *New York Times*, ten professional ball clubs from Boston to Baltimore responded to the call of the Brooklyn Excelsiors Club and assembled at the Club's rooms on Fulton Street "with a view of redeeming the national game from the odium attached to it by the evils introduced under the abuses of the worst phases of professional ball playing." The next night at Collier's Rooms on Broadway in Manhattan, they founded the National Association of Professional Base Ball Players.

From its beginnings, the National Association was also plagued by shady improprieties. Professional gamblers openly plied their trade at the ballparks, shouting out odds on batters. Albert Spalding bemoaned the status quo:

> For myself, I felt that the time was ripe for a change. Moreover, I was heartily disgusted with what I saw going on all about us. I knew that gambling was practiced everywhere; that such players as had not stamina to resist the overtures made to them were being caused to swerve from the legitimate ends of the game, and to serve the illegitimate purposes of the gamesters.

It was a time of self-aggrandizement in America, and the ballplayers were not going to be left out. Players "revolved" from club to club, often in mid-season, in order to increase their monthly wages.

The 1870s was a decade of economic growth and moral decay. The looting of peacetime America by public and private figures proceeded unabated. General Grant was in the White House and his cronies were in charge of the government. Entrepreneurial bandits pursued financial plunder with little public accountability. It was, the *Cincinnati Enquirer* wrote, "a decaying age of trade and swap." The commercialism of American life had become a nationwide hustle.

The Whiskey Ring, a conspiracy of Republican politicians and whiskey distillers from the Midwest, looted over three million dollars in taxes from the federal treasury, employing what the *Boston Globe* on May 13, 1875, called "a gigantic system of fraud":

> The work of purging out the corruption and bringing back once more a wholesome enforcement of law in this country is a task for Hercules, to which the task of cleaning the Augean stables was a pastime for a summer's day, but the assurances are strong and hopeful that it will be accomplished.

The extent of the Whiskey Ring's perfidy became clear in the months that followed. With the cooperation of bribed federal revenue officials, no excise taxes were paid on eighty percent of the whiskey shipped out of St. Louis. A portion of the take was funneled directly into Republican Party coffers. General Orville E. Babcock, Grant's private secretary, was indicted for his participation in the Ring. Forever loyal, Grant took the unprecedented step of offering testimony by way of deposition in support of his confidant. A jury of "honest farmers" acquitted him. Grant's Secretary of War, William Belknap, was not as fortunate. Investigated by a House committee and unanimously impeached for taking over $24,000 in bribes in exchange for the sale of Indian trading post positions, Belknap resigned his post in disgrace.

The National League

Looking back years later at the circumstances baseball faced in the mid-1870s, a committee of owners reported:

> Interest in base ball was at low ebb. Gamblers were in possession. The game was without discipline, organization or legitimate control. The sport was conducted with dishonest methods and for dishonest purposes, and had neither the respect nor confidence of the press or public. Heroic methods were absolutely necessary.

On February 2, 1876, eight club owners met in secret in New York City to take those "heroic methods." Energetic Chicago coal merchant William Hulbert called the meeting, inspired by Chicago Tribune editor Lewis Meecham. The professional teams in the National Association had little financial backing — seventeen clubs had announced their intention to join the Association in 1876 for the ten dollar entrance fee — and Hulbert was concerned that the organization would never be profitable. Hulbert claimed that a sternly-regulated, owner-operated circuit would provide the clean entertainment both spectators and good players wanted:

> Pool sellers and bookies would have to be kept out of the ballparks. Private police would be hired by the new league to rout gamblers from their seats and throw them into the streets. No

longer would drunkenness among players be tolerated, nor would players be permitted to tear up their contracts in mid-season and jump to another team.

Hulbert and his starting pitcher, Albert Spalding, wrote the first constitution for the new circuit. Each club owner reserved the power to ban from the game any of his players who engaged in dishonest activities. More importantly, the league president — Hulbert himself at the league's inception — could act to ban reprobates who contaminated the sport. The *Chicago Tribune* hailed the new era that would end "drunken behavior" and promote "honest play." Hulbert banned all alcoholic beverages from the ballparks: "Ladies and children must be allowed to view the competition in a dignified atmosphere," he explained to his fellow owners. The creation of the National League of Professional Baseball Clubs by eight club owners in 1876 offered a new opportunity to eliminate gambling, thrown contests and other disreputable conduct. Hulbert ordered all players in the new league to "stay clear of anyone known to be tied in with gambling circles. Such practices only detract from the magnificence of our teams."

Not all observers thought the replacement of the National Association by the National League would clean the slate. Father Chadwick, writing in the *New York Clipper*, considered Hulbert's coup d'état a "blunder" in the important work of reform. These were not "men of experience" who could

> put a stop to the growing abuses connected with their class of the baseball fraternity, the most prominent of which is the evil of fraudulent play in the form of "hippodroming," or the "selling" or "throwing" of games for betting purposes, practiced by knavish members of the club-teams, and countenanced by still worse club officials.

This reform movement, Chadwick lamented, would certainly fail. "The evil in question has begun to sap at the very foundations of the national game." Chadwick would be proved prescient.

Albert Spalding retired from playing baseball after only four games of the 1877 season — he had a record of 47 wins and 12 losses in 1876 — and devoted his full time to managing and promoting the business of the game. His first annual "official guide" pledged that the National League would "make base ball playing respectable and honorable." In an era when American business knew no limits to its nefarious schemes and manipulations, it was a promise that would be hard to fulfill, especially because the players whose misconduct had polluted the game during the years of the National Association were not banned from participating in the new National League venture. Yet Spalding naively believed in the essential goodness of ballplayers: "[I]t is just as natural for a ball player to play his best to win as it is for a duck to swim."

The Louisville Malefaction

As the president of the National League, William Hulbert's resolve to run professional baseball as a clean and attractive business venture would soon be tested by baseball's premier crime of the nineteenth century. The infamous Louisville caper of 1877 would rival the 1919 Black Sox as the worst scandal in baseball history. There were precursors to the corruption of the Louisville nine almost from the inception of the new circuit.

On May 27, 1876, the first year of National League play, the New York Mutuals triumphed over the St. Louis Browns 6–2 aided by three suspicious throwing errors in the first inning and one error in the second inning by second baseman Mike McGreary that produced all the Mutuals' runs. The *New York Times* reported that McGreary muffed "a pretty fly ball" and then threw at least ten feet over the catcher's head. St. Louis did not "seem to try to very hard, their fielding being less spirited than that usually displayed by them, while at the bat they did not accomplish anything of note." Infielder McGreary's career in the defunct National Association had featured many similar questionable outings. Although suspended after the game pending further investigation by Vice President C. O. Bishop of the St. Louis club, McGreary quickly returned to the Browns uniform. He would continue his major league

On a road trip east, the league-leading Louisville Grays lost a series of games under very suspicious circumstances. In fact, four of the stars of the club had taken bribes to throw the National League pennant, baseball's greatest scandal of the nineteenth century.

career, which included many other questionable performances, until retiring in 1882.

Not all schemes to fix the outcomes of games proved successful, but they certainly should have given warning as to what would lie ahead. One of the conspirators who would besmirch the game in 1877 aborted a similar plot during the 1876 season. George Bechtel, who had already been suspended by the Louisville Grays for "suspicious play" on May 30, 1876, telegraphed teammate James Devlin on June 10 with an offer of $500 if the club would lose that day's game against Boston. Devlin responded: "I want you to understand that I am not that kind of man." He reported the scheme to team management. The next season, Devlin would prove that he was that kind of man.

As the second season of the National League began in 1877, hopes were high for Hulbert's new circuit. On April 1, 1877, however, umpire Dan Devinney publicly charged that George McManus, the manager of the St. Louis franchise, had approached him for assistance in helping the Browns club beat the Louisville Grays. McManus, Devinney claimed, had offered him $250. McManus denied the accusation and nothing came of it. However, it did foreshadow the corruption that would infect the game later that season.

Throughout most of the summer of 1877, the Louisville Grays dominated their National League opponents, winning more than two out of every three games. Louisville's club owner, Charles Chase, had assembled a stellar group of players for the 1877 campaign, including ace pitcher James "Terror" Devlin, shortstop William "Butcher" Craver, outfielder "Gentleman" George Hall and, in mid-season, third baseman Al "Slippery Elm" Nichols. Alfred H. Nichols had begun his baseball career playing for the New York Mutuals, the Tammany Hall club.

By August 13, the club had built up a solid 3½ game lead with 12 games to go. The season was only 50 games long and the Grays were destined for the pennant. Starting in late August, however, the club's fortunes suddenly slipped dramatically. On a road trip east, Louisville lost a series of games under very suspicious circumstances. Star hurler Devlin, who pitched all 61 games for the Grays that season, lost his proficiency. His pitches lost their bite. Normally a steady hitter, Devlin repeatedly struck out. The team could not prevail in any of its contests against Hartford, Boston or even lowly last-place Cincinnati, losing seven in a row. The *Louisville Courier-Journal* suspected duplicity.

Although the Grays began to win some matches, the Red Stockings of Boston had secured the pennant by September 30. When the league championship was decided, the Grays began to win contests consistently, prevailing in all but one of its remaining games. After the close of the season the *Courier-Journal* dropped hints that all had not been "on the level" with the Louisville nine. The newspaper reported that the stars had been seen around town sporting diamond stick pins and rings.

During the disastrous eastern road trip, the *Courier-Journal* had run the headline "What's the Matter?" Club president Charles Chase had received anonymous telegrams from the east confirming that betting on the underdog Hartford club had been unusually strong. Chase confronted outfielder George Hall. Hall thought that Jim Devlin had already confessed, so he sought clemency and offered a full confession. Hall revealed his involvement in the fix, but blamed everything on the former Mutuals' third baseman Al Nichols. Nichols, in turn, revealed his contact with a gambler named James McCloud, who had offered Devlin and Hall $100 to throw an exhibition game in Cincinnati. (Hall, it seemed, also had his own contact with Brooklyn gambler Frank Powell, his brother-in-law.) Team captain Bill Craver was implicated only when he refused to allow president Chase to examine the Western Union telegrams he had sent and received. Chase eventually reviewed the paper trail of telegrams that confirmed the complicity of Devlin, Hall and Nichols in the scheme.

The directors of the Louisville ball club met on October 30, 1877, and announced the expulsion from baseball of Devlin, Hall, Craver and Nichols. Investigations had uncovered further evidence of thrown games throughout the eastern road trip. Craver was expelled for "disobedience of positive orders, general misconduct, and suspicious play in violation of his contract and the rules of the league." The formal charges against Devlin, Hall and Nichols were for "selling games, conspiring to sell games, and tampering with players."

The *Courier-Journal* rightfully took credit for the club's disciplinary actions. Much of the investigation had been done by its sportswriter, John A. Haldeman, the son of the club owner John Haldeman and the nephew of club president Charles Chase. The newspaper extolled management's ultimate decision: "As may well be imagined, the directors felt they had a most unpleasant task to perform but their duty to the League, to their own club, to themselves and to the integrity of the game left them no alternative."

Long before they were expelled, Devlin, Hall and Craver had announced that they would not be returning to the Louisville club for the 1878 season. (The league would not institute its "reserve system" until 1879, and the Louisville players were free to move from club to club when their contracts expired.) Except for little-used infielder Nichols, the Grays lost nothing by severing the four players from the game. It could even be argued that by expelling these players from baseball, management's action actually aided the prospects of its Louisville club. Now no other club would be able to field a team with these strong athletes. Whatever advantage the club might have gained, however, was short-lived.

League president Hulbert saw the Louisville scandal as the opportunity to prove his commitment to clean play in the National League. At its annual meeting in December, league officials ratified the actions of the Louisville club, banning the four players from the game for life. Two of the conspirators — Devlin and Hall — had been genuine stars of the game at the time. Devlin was a splendid pitcher who compiled at 35–25 record in 1877 with a 2.25 earned-run average. Hall was one of the game's great sluggers, the home run king of the new league. Their banishment sent a strong message: if you engage in "hippodroming," you will never play in the National League again. Spalding regaled this "first great victory won over gambling and the gamblers."

The St. Louis club, which had already signed Devlin and Hall to play for the 1878 campaign, was decimated by the National League's action. As a result, the club dropped out of the league until 1883. Having rid itself of its own finest players (who it was going to lose in any case) and unable to recruit adequate substitutes, the Louisville Grays also disbanded the franchise. The *Courier-Journal* blamed "the rascality of last year's players and the general conviction that dishonest players on other clubs were more the rule than the exception." Louisville, among the nation's largest cities at the time, would not have a professional baseball franchise for five years.

For the most part, following the Louisville calumny the game remained free from material taint for the remainder of the century. Gambling did not disappear, however, and we only know of scandals that became public. For example, in 1879, the Albany Capital Citys were accused on fixing games, and T. H. Murnane had to write to the *New York Clipper* to refute this "slander." On the other hand, there were some notable examples of public propriety. In 1888, baseball umpire John Kelly refused a $10,000 payoff to make sure that Boston bested the Providence club. As a result, he was thereafter referred to as "Honest John" Kelly. Cashing in on his reputation, he proceeded to open his own gambling establishment on 46th Street in New York City in the 1890s. Similarly, when Chicago gambler James S. Woodruff tried to bribe Cleveland Blues catcher and outfielder John Clapp in 1881, Clapp turned him in to police authorities, also earning the sobriquet "Honest John" in the process.

Henry Chadwick, baseball's premier scribe, waxed eloquently in 1882 in the pages of the *New York Clipper*, about the former "rottenness of the professional fraternity." The "crookedness," he claimed, was now supplanted by "an era of quietness" under "honest auspices."

Not all persons associated with the game stayed clean, however. One notorious crook was Dick Higham, who had a history of throwing games as a player in the National Association. Hired as an umpire, Higham worked closely with gambler James Todd to place bets on the games he would work. When an incriminating letter was intercepted by investigating detectives, Higham was barred from the game. He moved to Chicago to become a bookmaker. By all accounts, Higham is the only umpire in the history of the game to have been involved in fixing games.

It is too facile to try to explain away the dishonesty of some ballplayers on the grounds that they were pawns in an owner-controlled industry. As professionals, baseball players were generally well compensated for their play, although with nothing like modern salaries. The relationship between a player and his team, however, was decidedly one-sided. Under the boilerplate contract each player was required to sign, the player had "no claim for wages" if he were injured. Players were charged thirty dollars for their uniforms and required to maintain them themselves. Clubs also charged their players fifty cents a day for meals provided on the road.

On the other hand, baseball players were paid well when compared with the average working men of the time, earning at least seven times the median annual salary for a work obligation that took little more than half the year. The players came from working class backgrounds, often the sons or grandsons of immigrants, and their good fortune to play professionally was a substantial financial benefit. It seems fair to conclude that their occasional misdeeds were the product of greed, rather than some justified effort to redress their grievances. Yet, their transgressions cannot be seen as out-of-step with contemporary America. They rigged baseball while robber barons rigged railroad tariffs and city bosses collected graft. None of these acts were excusable. They were all cut from the same cloth.

Robber Barons

Baseball's 1877 misdemeanors commanded the attention of the public, but the stern discipline meted out to the Louisville Four effectively stemmed the tide of scandal, at least for a while. On the other hand, the Gilded Age of post-Civil War America brought untold riches to those willing and able to play the fast and lawless game of business. These were ruthless and corrupt men. Nothing seemed to stem the tide of their collusion and avarice, even federal laws and criminal trials. By comparison, the baseball scandals were just a small-time delinquency.

The Civil War offered abundant opportunities for profit unlike anything seen before in America. Those who could quickly supply material needed to prosecute that war — cannon and food, mostly — did not need to be too concerned about the quality of their merchandise. The Federal Government had opened its checkbook — actually its bond financing — and agile businessmen profited from the terrible conflagration. While those unable to buy their way out of service with the $300 bounty marched off to battle, entrepreneurs followed the first imperative of America — making money. These mercenaries for profit became America's ruling economic class.

America's postwar industrialization created enormous concentrations of unregulated and untaxed wealth for those who offered an answer to the nation's central problem: How do you create a continental market? First build a railroad. Actually, build many railroads, many more than the country needed, and make sure all were subsidized by public assets. Most great fortunes after the Civil War were made in or around the railroads. Railroads and their operators created an industrial system that made America the richest country in the world.

Although many aspired to gain riches, only a few succeeded in taking full advantage of the opportunities the new economy offered. These amoral pragmatists — Leland Stanford, C. P. Huntington, Jay Gould, E. H. Harriman, James J. Hill and "Jubilee Jim" Fisk, among others — were men of great organizational ability. They were also ruthless and dishonest without apparent limitation. Fisk, the organizer of the Erie Railroad, even organized a baseball club in 1870 to compete for the public's attention with the dominant Mutuals club of Boss Tweed. Fisk was more successful as a railroad man.

They pushed others aside in their rise to the business aristocracy. "Commodore" Vanderbilt when asked about whether his manipulations might violate the law, responded: "Law! What do I care about the Law! Hain't I got the power?"

Railroads demanded public land concessions in exchange for laying track. As a result, railroads owned a significant portion of the best unsettled land in America. The companies would extort as much in freight rates from private customers as the traffic would allow. They would issue watered stock, crash their own companies and fight their rivals without bounds. Milton Hannibal Smith, the president of the Louisville and Nashville Railroad for forty years, explained the corporatist philosophy: "Society as created was for the purpose of one man's getting what the other fellow has, if he can, and keep out of the penitentiary."

The robber barons manipulated financial markets and, when necessary, corrupted state and federal officials. Freed of the constraints of enforced law, their financial schemes lined their own pockets. They were then honored for having succeeded at the American contest. On occasion they would work in concert to eliminate a joint rival, and then turn against each other when the terms of the battle had changed. These tycoons saw their role in American society as the product of divine providence — John D. Rockefeller said: "God gave me my money." They spent their fabulous wealth on gaudy luxuries. Jay Gould slept in a $25,000 bed. J. P. Morgan purchased his own $100,000 rail car. Collis Huntington built a $2,000,000 mansion.

The Credit Mobilier scheme of 1872 is a splendid example of the state of America's business morals at the same time baseball was cementing its hold as the national pastime. Stockholders in the Union Pacific Railroad Company created a dummy corporation, the Credit Mobilier, to construct its portion of the continental railroad. They bribed Congressmen by selling stock at below market rates to legislators in exchange for favorable votes on pending legislation supplying government subsidies. The Union Pacific paid the Credit Mobilier $73 million for $50 million worth of work, the difference going to the directors of the construction company who were also the directors of the railroad. When the *New York Sun* broke the story of the plot in 1872, a few Congressmen were censured, but no politicians or businessmen served prison time.

These entrepreneurial "malefactors of great wealth," as Teddy Roosevelt would later call them, saw the accumulation of these ill-gotten riches as a game to be played by rules that they set and changed at will. Jay Gould, for example, was a scoundrel of the first rank. He pieced together a railroad monopoly, owning the Wabash, Union Pacific, Southern Pacific, Denver Pacific, Texas Pacific, Kansas Pacific and the Missouri Pacific railroads, among others. From 1872 until his death in 1892, he was a director of seventeen lines and the president of five. His stock manipulation of the Erie Railroad fleeced that company dry and left his fellow stockholders penniless. Gould owned the New York World newspaper and the Associated Press. He would smear a corporation, driving down the price, then purchase the target company at a reduced price, loot its assets, restore its reputation using the media and then sell it. Gould employed a private army of bodyguards and security personnel to insure his personal safety. His manipulation of the economy caused untold misery for ordinary workers, but Gould was not afraid: "I can hire one-half of the working class to kill the other half." Eventually, it was other business magnates, not the unwashed urban dwellers, who took Gould down.

These business magnates came from common backgrounds and built their wealth by any means possible. Commodore Vanderbilt, for example, was born on a farm on Staten Island, and he never learned to spell. Jay Gould was also the son of a farmer from upstate New York. Andrew Carnegie was the immigrant son of a Scottish weaver who grew up in the slums of Pittsburgh. The business aristocracy lived at a time when unschooled intelligence and rapaciousness, audacity and boldness, and heresy and lawlessness paid big dividends. They wouldn't steal second base; they would steal the whole stadium and the town in which it sat.

Although criminal activity by business tycoons was not unusual, it was also not universal. Thomas Edison, Ezra Cornell, Samuel Morse, John Jacob Astor, the Wright Brothers, and many others earned substantial sums without running afoul of legal or moral principles. Most baseball players played by the rules as well, gave to the contests their best efforts, and succeeded by virtue of the merits of the competition.

Gambling, Politics and Baseball

With the establishment of the American League in 1901 and its merger in 1903 with the National League, organized baseball assumed the sixteen-club structure that would carry it through the first half of the twentieth century. Garry Herrmann, the well-liked owner of the Cincinnati Redlegs, chaired the three-man National Commission. Despite his official title, Herrmann remained firmly under the control of George B. Cox, Cincinnati's political boss, and American League president Ban Johnson. Under the National Commission, baseball players continued their well-established pattern of fixing ballgames.

Based on the sport's prior history, newspapers regularly raised allegations of misdoing. On other occasions, newspapers would spout baseball's official mantra that the game was beyond reproach. The *Washington Post* on August 28, 1904, assured its readers:

Occasionally, one hears the accusation made against a player by some rapid fan that he is "trying to throw the game," in other words, trying to make his side lose. There was a time when such a thing was possible in baseball, but it can't be practiced now. . . . [A]s soon as a manager sees that one of his men is not working up to standard he immediately supplants him with another, this being especially true of pitchers.

Notwithstanding such assurances, the close connection between baseball and the gambling establishment continued. This nexus would eventually cause the Black Sox catastrophe.

Baseball also had direct links to corrupt politicians. Andrew Freedman, owner of the National League New York Giants at the turn of the century, was a Tammany Hall crony of Boss Crocker, a notable successor to master racketeer Boss Tweed. A despicable man, Freedman, reported the *Sporting News*, "had an arbitrary disposition, a violent temper, and an ungovernable tongue in anger which was easily provoked and he was disposed to be arbitrary to the point of tyranny with subordinates." Freedman appreciated the threat posed by the rival American League and, using his powerful Tammany connections, announced that a street would be built through any plot of land designated for an American League ballpark. After eight years in the national game, Freedman in 1902 sold the Giants ball club to John T. Brush for $200,000 to devote his full attention to plundering the construction contracts for New York's new subway system.

In 1903, American League president Ban Johnson relocated the league's Baltimore club to New York and handpicked big-time gambler Frank Farrell and police commissioner "Big Bill" Devery as the owners of the new Highlanders. They paid $18,000 for the franchise. Farrell, Devery and Crocker's successor as Tammany boss, Tim Sullivan, controlled numerous Manhattan gambling venues, and their combined clout counteracted the political effort by Giants manager John McGraw and Giants owner Farrell to deny the Highlanders land on which to construct a ball field. Farrell and Devery kept the Highlanders club for ten lack-luster years and sold the franchise for $460,000 to a pair of colonels, Jake Ruppert, the brewer, and Tillinghast Huston, a contractor and engineer. Ruppert was also a long-time Tammany official.

In 1912, Charles Stoneham, a shady financier and a secret partner of gambling kingpin Arnold Rothstein, purchased the National Exhibition Company, the operating company of the New York Giants club and ably used his own Tammany connections to aid his franchise's prospects. McGraw, who was a regular gambler in the off season, became part owner of the Giants he managed and the club's vice president. The other part owner was Judge Francis X. McQuade, another longtime crony of gambler Arnold Rothstein. McQuade served as treasurer of the club, outside employment for a judge that was in open violation of state law that required that a magistrate "devote his whole time and capacity, so far as the public interest demands, to the duties of his office." At the same time that Stoneham, McGraw and McQuade bought the Giants, they also purchased a racetrack and casino in Havana.

Waddell, Zimmerman, Chase and the Lead-up to the 1919 Black Sox

In the 1905 World Series, the Philadelphia Athletics were without the service of their ace left-handed hurler George Edward "Rube" Waddell. Waddell was generally referred to in the newspapers as "eccentric" and for good reason. He turned cartwheels going from the mound to the bench. In one exhibition game, he called in his outfielders and proceeded to strike out the opponents on nine straight pitches. He would vanish in the middle of a game to chase fire engines. He wrestled alligators in a Florida circus in the off-season for two dollars a performance. He was a notorious drinker. His two marriages ended when his wives left him. (Waddell also forgot to divorce his first wife before marrying his second.)When first acquired by the Athletics, owner Connie Mack decided it was a wise investment to send two Pinkerton guards to Los Angeles to escort his new pitcher to the east coast. Waddell, a big, lanky left-hander, was very strange, but was he crooked?

The newspapers were quick to blame Waddell's mysterious 1905 injury on gamblers and to claim that it was a bribe that had "disabled" the star pitcher. One report even had the gamblers feting Waddell in a

New York City hotel surrounded by showgirls. Waddell said he had hurt his shoulder while wrestling with teammate Andy Coakley at a train station. (The rumor was that Waddell had objected to Coakley's wearing a straw hat out of season. There is no other historical evidence of Rube's sartorial sensitivities.) The Athletics lost the series to the New York Giants in five games. Many years later, Horace Fogel, the president of the Philadelphia Phillies, told a newspaper that New York gambler Tim Sullivan had offered Waddell $17,000 to stay out of the 1905 series, but ended up paying the pitcher only $500. Nothing was ever proven, except that real and imagined fixes were deeply imbedded in the ethos of the national game.

In the 1905 World Series, the Philadelphia Athletics were without the service of their ace left-handed hurler George Edward "Rube" Waddell. Newspapers blamed his mysterious 1905 injury on gamblers who bribed the future member of the Hall of Fame.

Some players resisted attempts at fixing contests. Lou Criger, Cy Young's personal catcher with the 1903 Boston Americans, reported to American League President Ban Johnson twenty years later that a gambler named Anderson had offered him a bribe of $12,000 to affect the outcome of the first World Series. (He was to share the money with Young.) Some who had observed the first game of that series wondered whether Criger had actually declined the bribe. He played quite poorly as the Pirates initially triumphed, before falling to Boston five games to three.

Another notorious incident preceding the infamous 1919 Black Sox fix occurred in 1908, when the New York Giants team physician attempted to affect the outcome of the club's one game playoff against the Chicago Cubs. Dr. Joseph Creamer offered umpires Bill Klem and Jimmy Johnston $2,500 to ensure a victory for the Giants. The umpires refused the offer and reported Creamer's approach to the league office. National League president Harry Pulliam appointed a three-owner committee to investigate whether the Giants had tried to put in the fix. Remarkably, Pulliam appointed the owner of the New York Giants, John T. Brush, as chair of the committee! Based on the committee's report, which implicated no one else from the Giants in this scheme, Pulliam expelled Dr. Creamer from professional baseball for life. The *New York Evening Journal* asked in May 1909: "Who were the men behind Doctor Creamer?" No answer was ever supplied, even though the likely answer was that it was Giants manager John McGraw. There was also some evidence that even before this playoff game, the Giants had sought to secure a place in the post-season by an illegal payoff. Agents tried to bribe the Philadelphia Phillies with $40,000 to throw a five-game series in late September of that year.

By the 1910s, gambling and game fixing (both attempted and actual) was occurring with regularity at the major league level. Ballplayers, such as Heinie Zimmerman and Hal Chase, were regularly seen in the company of gamblers. Zimmerman, an outstanding third baseman with the Cubs and Giants from 1907–1919, led the league in batting, hits, doubles and home runs in 1912. He developed a reputation as a bad actor, however. According to the *Sporting News*, Zimmerman was a player whose "energy was misdirected and talents largely wasted." The Cubs dealt him to the Giants, where manager McGraw thought he could rehabilitate the player. In 1919, McGraw suspended Zimmerman for throwing games and bribing others to do so, ending his baseball career. (The *New York Times* article on November 13, 1919, simply reported that "Zim" would be missing from the Giants for the 1920 season because he was "tired of the big leagues.") In an affidavit in 1921, Zimmerman admitted to being a go-between for gamblers. He told Giants players Fred

Toney, Rube Benton and Benny Kauff that they would be paid off if the New York club lost. After leaving baseball, Zimmerman became a partner with Dutch Schultz in a New York City speakeasy.

"Prince" Hal Chase had an even more notorious side to his otherwise stylish career as a ballplayer. Perhaps baseball's finest first baseman of his era — sportswriter Frederick Lieb called him "the premier first sacker . . . since the time of Adam"— Chase also could have been the most egregious baseball criminal of all time. He had a propitious start to his career, batting .323 in his sophomore year with the New York Highlanders. In 1907, *Sporting Life* called Chase "modest in the extreme, well balanced, level headed, educated youth, whose habits are above reproach." Starting in 1908, however, rumors began to circulate that Chase was "laying down" to affect the outcome of some contests. By 1910, his manager with the Yankees, George Stallings, publicly accused Chase of throwing games, but club president Frank Farrell and league president Ban Johnson dismissed the allegations. For good measure, the Yankees fired Stallings and replaced him with Hal Chase, who proceeded to run the franchise down to sixth place in his one year at the helm.

Unlike some other moral degenerates in the long history of the game, Chase was not a short-term felon. Wherever he went during his fifteen-year major league career, rumors surfaced about his questionable activities. He developed a well-earned reputation for corruption as a "bad actor." The Yankees finally traded him in 1913 after manager Frank Chance became convinced of his duplicity. Joe Vila of the *New York Sun* later called Chase "a genius gone to ruin."

Chase continued to play, however, first for the White Sox and then for Buffalo in the short-lived Federal League. Finally, in 1916 Chase signed with the Cincinnati Reds. The longtime owner of the Cincinnati Reds, Garry Hermann, and his manager, the "Christian Gentleman" Christy Mathewson, brought public charges against Chase in 1918, claiming he colluded with gamblers to throw games. National League president John Heydler held a hearing on January 30, 1919. At the day-long affair, depositions were received from manager Mathewson, then serving with the American armed forces in Europe, and Giant pitcher

Pol Perritt, who claimed that Chase had approached him with a "mysterious proposition." Chase testified in his own behalf and impressed the league president.

On February 5, 1919, Heydler dismissed the accusation that Chase had bet against his team in games in which he played, deciding that Chase's substandard play in the field was due to mere "carelessness" and that he otherwise acted in a "foolish manner." Chase's "careless talk" created "an atmosphere of distrust" among his Cincinnati teammates. He was just talking in a "joking spirit" that was construed otherwise. There was no evidence presented of intentional misconduct on his part in violation of league rules:

> My conclusion and finding, after full consideration of the evidence, is that it is nowhere established that the accused was interested in any pool or wager that caused any game of ball to result otherwise than on its merits, and that player Hal H. Chase is not guilty of the charges brought against him.

Chase had admitted making only two bets on baseball, one many years previously and a second in 1917 when he bet on his own team to prevail. President Heydler warned all ballplayers that forthwith anyone who placed a bet on a game would be barred from the sport forever. The exoneration of Chase, whose long history of misdeeds was generally well known, gave impetus and encouragement to those who would scar the integrity of the game that fall during the 1919 World Series. The Reds refused to reemploy Chase and traded him to McGraw and the Giants. McGraw was confident he could rehabilitate Chase, but he had met his match.

Chase was a criminal who earned a good living cheating at the game he knew how to play so well. After one final season in 1919 with the Giants, he was officially "retired" from the game, along with other questionable players, Heinie Zimmerman and Lee McGee. Chase maintained his connections to the gamblers, however. On his death bed in May 1947, he admitted that he had known about the Black Sox fix in the planning stages. He was approached by Bill Burns with a proposition to earn a lot of money. He said he turned down the offer, but later regretted his failure to tell league president Heydler about it. (He did not want to be a "welcher.") In fact, he was in on the 1919 Black Sox fix (some suggest he even conceived of the entire scheme) and won $40,000 betting on that series: "I can't figure why managers and club fixers couldn't see the handwriting on the wall." Chase moved west after leaving the major leagues, and tried to bribe a Pacific Coast League pitcher to throw a ballgame in Los Angeles. The Chicago grand jury that indicted the Black Sox also named Chase, but he eluded extradition from California and nothing was ever proved against him.

Hal Chase continued to play semi-professional baseball under various names until he was fifty, and even on the sandlots he was considered a crooked player. His obituary in the *New York Times* on July 18, 1947, euphemistically termed Chase a "rough-and-tumble" ballplayer. Actually, he was just a crook and an outcast, deliberately losing games to win bets or payoffs.

The entrepreneurs who ran the game helped perpetuate the shameful environment that eventually led to the sport's great cataclysm, the fixing of the 1919 World Series. As sports columnist I. E. Sanburn wrote in the *Chicago Tribune* on September 12, 1920:

> Procrastination has proven the thief of something more valuable than time in the case of professional baseball versus gambling. It has cost the game a considerable portion of its good reputation. ... If the promoters of professional baseball had heeded the warning dinned into their ears for years against the inroads of the betting fraternity on their business, they would have headed off much of the trouble that has come to them, and which still is coming to them.

Sanburn particularly pointed to the lenient treatment of Chase as a forerunner of trouble for the National Game.

It is hard to justify what Chase and others did, but the club owners must bear a full measure of the responsibility. Although the business was quite profitable, owners paid players modest wages and quickly replaced any player who chaffed under such treatment. At the same time, owners who gambled could easily arrange for their clubs to perform brilliantly one day, but not the next. It was a recognized custom throughout much of baseball's history for owners to offer their underpaid players "incentive payments" to win particular contests. This questionable practice — banned under today's player contracts — fostered special effort and increased the winning chances for a bettor. Pitchers on losing clubs were offered incentives to prevail against contending clubs during a pennant race. The payoffs for the gamblers were substantial, while the owners gave their players a new dress suit.

Perfidy

With the race tracks closed during the First World War, gamblers turned their attention and their dollars to baseball. First among them was New York's Arnold Rothstein. Rothstein was involved in the importation and distribution of illegal drugs and alcohol, loan sharking and racketeering, fencing stolen jewelry and bookmaking. On the side, he fixed and bet on baseball games. One would think that the connection between baseball and notorious gamblers like Arnold Rothstein would be very troubling to baseball officials. In fact, although the evidence supported the inference that Rothstein had bankrolled the Black Sox venture of 1919, League President Johnson expressed his full confidence in Rothstein's innocence after meeting face-to-face with the gambling entrepreneur: "He did admit to me that he's heard of the fixing, but in spite of that, declared he had wagered on the White Sox." Rothstein did openly wager minor amounts on the Chicago American League club, but just to cover his tracks. He also won enormous sums by using stringers to place bets on the National League Reds.

When called before the Chicago grand jury that later indicted eight White Sox ballplayers, Rothstein testified:

The whole thing started when (Abe) Attell and some other cheap gamblers decided to frame the Series and make a killing. The world knows I was asked in on the deal and my friends know how I turned it down flat. I don't doubt that Attell used my name to put it over. That's been done by smarter men than Abe. But I wasn't in on it, wouldn't have gone into it under any circumstances and didn't bet a cent on the Series after I found out what was underway. My idea was that whatever way things turned out, it would be a crooked Series anyhow and that only a sucker would bet on it.

Rothstein was far too modest in relating his role.

Some who watched the premier Chicago White Sox lose the 1919 Series, including Chicago reporter Hugh Fullerton, sensed that certain star players had failed to meet their usual level of playing excellence, but most knew that even the best club in baseball could disappoint its fans on some occasions. Baseball is, after all, the most difficult team sport to play. Ring Lardner, the author and sportswriter, rode on the Sox private railroad car. He sensed the games were not on the level. He entertained his fellow journalists with this parody of "I'm forever blowing bubbles":

> I'm forever blowing ball games
> Pretty ball games in the air.
> I come from Chi,
> I hardly try,
> Just go to bat and fade and die.
> Fortunes coming my way,
> That's why I don't care.
> I'm forever blowing ball games
> And the gamblers treat us fair.

Not all sensed the fix. Billy Evans, who umpired the 1919 Series, later told the *Sporting News*: "Well, I guess I'm just a big dope. That Series looked all right to me."

More troubling to observers than the ultimate outcome of the games was the sharp shift in the betting odds shortly before the start of the Series. The Sox had been highly favored and suddenly they became the betting underdog. Historians agree that the players' behavior on those days in October 1919 was not just the result of a group of ballplayers having a bad stretch simultaneously. It was the result of a conspiracy of players and gamblers.

The famous trial of the Black Sox that led to their acquittal on criminal charges is part of American legend. The perfidy dug deep into the national mythology. According to the *Chicago Herald and Examiner*, as "Shoeless Joe" Jackson left the courthouse in the Loop after testifying before the grand jury "one little urchin in the crowd grabbed him by the coat sleeve. 'It ain't true, is it?' he said. 'Yes, kid, I'm afraid it is,' Jackson replied. 'Well, I'd never have thought it,' the boy exclaimed."

Historians have tried to reconstruct the events of the conspiracy that led to the fixed series. All agree that Charles Comiskey, the owner of the White Sox, provoked the resentment of his players, underpaying his stars and breaking contract promises. The team had been nicknamed the "Black Sox" long before the events of 1919 because Comiskey would not wash their dirty uniforms.

That said, the conspiracy was a remarkable and sinister accomplishment in such a public enterprise as baseball's fall classic. It showed the same genius for organization that the robber barons had used to transform the American economy. First baseman Chick Gandil was the mastermind of the plot, but each of his co-conspirators had his own grievances against the imperious owner. They were also greedy and crooked. Gandil first approached the Sox' leading hurler Eddie Cicotte. Much in debt and nearing the end of his career, Cicotte eventually listened to Gandil's entreaties. Gandil sought out the key infielder, shortstop Swede Risberg. Gandil needed one more pitcher to make the plot work, and he enticed Lefty Williams to participate.

Gandil almost was able to keep the conspiracy secret. Utility infielder Fred McMullin, Risberg's friend, overheard a conversation between Gandil and Risberg, and so he was included. Although he did not need them to pull off his crime, Gandil also enticed Joe Jackson and Happy Felsch to join the plot. Buck Weaver, the Sox premier third baseman, was approached, but he later denied ever agreeing to participate. The remaining White Sox — including future Hall of Famers second baseman Eddie Collins and catcher Ray Schalk — were kept far from the conspiracy, although they sensed their teammates were "laying down." Any of them might have informed management and blown the criminal enterprise, but it is also likely that Comiskey himself already knew exactly what was happening.

Gandil needed a source of capital for his plot to succeed, and there were gamblers aplenty ready to participate. He approached his old friend from Boston "Sport" Sullivan, who eventually received underwriting from Arnold Rothstein. His later denials notwithstanding, Rothstein funded the criminal enterprise. There were double-crosses and misdealings along the way, but the dye was cast.

In his splendid biography of Rothstein, David Pietrusza lays out the evidence that two sets of gamblers were involved in the fix, but it ultimately was the threat of violence against pitcher Lefty Williams that completed the cabal. Some of the players saw some money, but nothing like they had been promised. The Sox's manager, Kid Gleason, knew the conspirators were taking a dive and told Comiskey, who in turn told American League President Ban Johnson. Johnson dismissed the tale as scurrilous. The fix almost fell apart when gamblers who were losing money when Chicago lost attempted a reverse fix, by bribing key Cincinnati Reds players. They were unsuccessful.

After the White Sox lost the series, Charles Comiskey worked diligently to cover-up the perfidy. He proclaimed publicly that the series had been on the level and offered a $20,000 reward to anyone who could prove otherwise. When approached with proof, however, Comiskey brushed it aside.

Hugh Fullerton, the intrepid sports reporter for the *Chicago Herald and Examiner*, refused to allow the story to die, although his newspaper feared Comiskey's wrath. Much as reporter John A. Haldeman of the *Louisville Courier-Journal* unearthed baseball's great fixing scandal of 1877, Fullerton accumulated evidence of the conspiracy. He supplied his story to the *New York Evening World*, which on December 15, 1919, printed the reporter's circumstantial case. Eventually, the dam broke, the grand jury indicted the conspirators and baseball faced its Judgment Day. Remarkably, the confessions of three ballplayers before the grand jury had disappeared by the time of trial. After two hours and forty-seven minutes, the jury acquitted their local heroes and blamed the gamblers. On August 3, 1921, the day after the players were victorious in court, Commissioner Landis banned the eight Chicago Black Sox from baseball for life.

Although Landis' decision mirrored the action taken by William Hulbert in 1877 to ban the Louisville Four, some saw his punishment as cruel. Fans did not want to believe their heroes could be such villains. After all, a jury had acquitted the alleged conspirators and not all the participants were equally at fault. Yet, when seen in light of decades of similar dealings between players and gamblers, Landis's penalty was proper.

The congenital corruption in baseball had been resistant to change, like a virus without a cure that would periodically resurface and debilitate the national game. If banning the Black Sox is seen simply as punishment for a single misdeed, the penalty may seem excessive at least for some of the players. Yet, Landis's action was taken not only to punish these players, but also to deter future misconduct of the same or similar type. No baseball player has missed the message. If you consort with gamblers, you will never play in the National Game again.

As he neared death as a result of a lifetime of alcohol abuse, Mickey Mantle, the great Yankee centerfielder, urged the youth of America not to follow his example.

Chapter 4

Alcohol, Drugs and the National Pastime

"I did not take steroids. Period."— Rafael Palmeiro

"Wake up the echoes at the Hall of Fame and you will find that baseball's immortals were a rowdy and raucous group of men who would climb down off their plaques and go rampaging through Cooperstown, taking spoils."— Bill Veeck

WE ELEVATE PROFESSIONAL ATHLETES to the status of heroes, yet they are not immune from the normal temptations of life. They drink, they carouse, they even use drugs that might enhance their performances and moderate their cares. We require these talented ballplayers, upon penalty of public censure, to be the modest embodiment of All-American virtues. One of the classiest players of all time, Christy Mathewson, expressed the player's perspective that it should be the game that counts and not a ballplayer's off-field behavior: "I owe everything I have to [the fans] when I'm out there on the mound. But I owe the fans nothing and they owe me nothing when I am not pitching." In fact, fans have always demanded a great deal from ballplayers, and they have often been disappointed.

Baseball players suffer the pains of a long season. Their livelihoods depend upon their continued ability to perform at the highest level of athletic excellence, even if their bodies need rest and recuperation. Drugs and alcohol offer a palliative. Baseball players have always displayed their human frailties. Alcohol and drug use in the national pastime tells us something about the temptations of American culture and the human condition.

The use of performance-enhancing substances is not a purely modern phenomenon. It is said that in Ancient Greece athletes would pulverize the testes of bulls, dogs and sheep and brew a tea that would improve their performance during the Olympic Games. Did Coroebus, the first Olympic sprint champion in 776 B.C., use substances to improve his performance? The historical record is unclear. We know that athletes who toured Greece ate strict protein diets to strengthen their muscle mass and combined various potions with mushrooms and plant seeds.

Nineteenth century athletes were fortified by numerous concoctions. Swimmers in Amsterdam's canal races in the 1860s were accused of using drugs to enhance their performances. French cyclists in 1879 were found to have used a simple caffeine stimulant and a Belgian team used ether-laced sugar cubes. Sprint cyclists also tried nitroglycerine. A British cyclist died in 1886 after using ephedrine. Many athletes in various sports used substances to dull pain. For example, boxers used a potent combination of alcohol and strychnine to reduce the pain, the inevitable by-product of their bare-knuckled, midday matches that would last for hours.

During the second half of the nineteenth century, athletes experimented with a variety of psychoactive compounds, alcoholic and caffeinated beverages, tobacco, opiates, cannabis, coca, cocaine and strychnine to improve their performance. By the end of that century, Americans had become the greatest coffee drinkers in the world, importing 40 percent of the world's supply, and American athletes appreciated the stimulation that caffeine offered.

Some efforts at enhancing athletic performance around the turn of the twentieth century proved quite dangerous. In 1896, a cyclist from South Wales died from an overdose of trimethyl in the Bordeaux-Paris cycling race. At the first American Olympic Games in 1904 in St. Louis, American marathon runner Thomas Hicks collapsed after ingesting a mixture of strychnine, brandy and water from a car radiator. His handlers helped him across the finish line to win the long-distance event.

Steroids in the Nineteenth Century

Twenty-first century baseball players have been subjected to public scorn and media insult for using performance-enhancing substances, in particular for ingesting or injecting anabolic steroids. Only a small handful of players have either admitted such use or tested positively for the drug, but goaded by Congressional grandstanding and presidential interference, this has all caused quite a public fury. Use of steroid-like substances, however, is not a modern phenomenon. It can be traced back to nineteenth-century baseball. In fact, at least one Hall-of-Fame pitcher of that era used a testosterone treatment to improve his performance.

In 1889, French-American physiologist Charles Brown-Sequard developed an extract derived from the testicles of a guinea pig and a dog and injected himself to test its efficacy. It was a simple formula:

Cut…testicles into four or five slices, mix with one liter of glycerine, store for twenty-four hours turning frequently, wash in boiling water, pass the liquid through a paper filter, and then sterilize at 104 degrees.

On June 1, 1889, Dr. Brown-Séquard presented a sensational report about his work at the Société de Biologie in Paris, where he served as the president, documenting his own rejuvenation after six injections of his potion. He claimed that he had "regained at least all the force which I possessed a number of years ago," conquering his constipation and regaining the intellectual vigor of his youth. (He even claimed to the startled audience that he had lengthened the arc of his urine stream by 25 percent so he could blast cockroaches off *la toilette* wall.) Brown-Séquard's potion was the first known modern treatment containing testosterone.

Word of Brown-Séquard's discovery spread rapidly and, reading the sensational headlines, the public was fascinated. Brown-Séquard was well known in the American medical community, having practiced, researched and taught in New York and Boston for many years. Unlike the many quack doctors who were ubiquitous in the nineteenth century, Brown-Séquard was a celebrated member of the American Academy of Arts and

Sciences, the National Academy of Sciences, the Royal Society, and the Academie des Sciences. The *Boston Globe* on July 4, 1889, hailed his new substance "that would rejuvenate the old and make strong the feeble."

Dr. Brown-Séquard explained that his elixir would build up the "nervous force" of ill patients by bolstering their strength and resistance. Former U.S. surgeon general, Dr. William Hammond, who practiced in Washington, reported that use of the Brown-Séquard's elixir reduced pain, improved cardiac function, and restored potency. The press was filled with testimonials in support of the treatment's effectiveness. Colonel William B. Lowe reported to the *Atlanta Constitution* that a celebrated French fencer who had become debilitated from "locomotor ataxia" underwent the Brown-Sequard treatment and "regained his health and strength . . . and when I called upon him, he was teaching a class of six the sword exercise. He held all six at bay, and jumped all around the hall in his maneuvers with all the agility of a boy of sixteen." The *Washington Post* suggested that this wholesome potion was "a most valuable and powerful stimulant."

By the end of 1889, more than 12,000 physicians had administered the Brown-Séquard's potion. The *Boston Globe* asked the most famous athlete of the day, heavyweight champion John L. Sullivan, about the Brown-Séquard elixir. He was well-acquainted with the treatment, but he was skeptical: "It may be some good, but I doubt it. You can never tell until you try." "La Méthode Sequardienne," the most celebrated stimulant of the era, was the precursor of modern anabolic steroids.

Given such glowing testimonials, it would not have been surprising if some aging professional baseball players were tempted to try the fabulous elixir. The press did not ignore the potential usefulness of the potion for baseball players. Within weeks after Brown-Sequard announced his discovery, the *New Haven Register* wrote:

> The discovery of a true elixir of youth by which the aged can restore their vitality and renew their bodily vigor would be a great thing for baseball nines. We hope the discovery . . . is of such a nature that it can be applied to rejuvenate provincial clubs.

The *Washington Post* on August 14, 1889, reported the use of the testosterone potion as a performance-enhancing substance by a major league baseball player:

> Galvin was one of the subjects at a test of the Brown-Séquard elixir at a medical college in Pittsburgh on Monday. If there still be doubting Thomases who concede no virtue in the elixir, they are respectfully referred to Galvin's record in yesterday's Boston-Pittsburgh game. It is the best proof yet furnished of the value of the discovery.

In the game following his treatment right-hander Jimmy Galvin shut out the Boston club 9–0. The *Washington Post* called it one of the "best games of his life." He was unusually prolific at bat. In the fourth inning, according to the *Pittsburgh Commercial Gazette*, "Galvin surprised the crowd by driving the ball into left field for two bases," batting in two runs. In the fifth inning

> When the old man stepped to the plate, he was greeted with a salvo of cheers, and cries of "hit her for a home run, Jimmy" could be heard all over the grounds. Galvin raised his cap and waited patiently until he got a nice slow ball. He caught it right on the end of his bat, and the sphere went sailing down over Johnson's head into the weeds in deep center field. When the crowd realized what he had done, they set up a shout, and the grandstands and bleachers fairly shook with the tremendous stamping of feet. When the ball was returned, Galvin was on third base, doffing his hat to the crowd, while Dunlop had scored another run.

The *Pittsburgh Commercial Gazette* confirmed that three physicians in the city — Dr. Chevalier Q. Jackson, Dr. H. A. Page and Dr. W. C. Byers — had been "experimenting with the animal injection." Dr. Page had injected three persons with the Brown-Sequard treatment on the day Galvin received his treatment. The Western Pennsylvania Medical College — likely the medical college referred to by the *Post*, because it was

Pittsburgh's James "Pud" Galvin used testosterone shots in 1889 to enhance his pitching performance as his Hall of Fame career neared its end.

the only such institution in Pittsburgh — had opened three years earlier on Brereton Avenue, about two miles from the ballpark where Galvin's National League club, then called the "Alleghenys," played their games.

James Francis Galvin had begun his professional baseball career in 1875. A product of the Irish Kerry Patch in St. Louis, he was recognized as the best amateur in the city. Signed by the St. Louis Reds, his teammates called him "Pud," because he made "pudding" of opposing batters. A short, stocky man with a handlebar moustache, Galvin was a work horse, known for his fast ball and pinpoint control. He was a tireless worker on the mound. By 1889 when he tried the testosterone potion, the "rotund twirler" of the Pittsburgh Alleghanys was 32 years old and his best playing days were over. The 1889 season was the last year he would be among the league's premier "twirlers." It is no wonder he would try the elixir, but it did not help him in the long run. Galvin aged quickly. The following year, the *Chicago Tribune* wrote: "Jimmy Galvin says he is only 33 years old. Jimmy must have gone to 40 and then started back in the count." Pittsburgh cut his salary in half. Galvin pitched a few more years and retired in 1892. Galvin umpired for a while and tended bar in Pittsburgh. He died penniless of a stomach disorder in 1902 at age 47, and his baseball friends raised money to cover his funeral expenses. Galvin, the first major league baseball player to accumulate 300 wins and the first known to have used a steroid-like substance to enhance his performance, was voted into the baseball Hall of Fame by the Veterans Committee in 1965.

The Battle Against Alcohol

Early entrepreneurs of the sport of baseball recognized the problematical relationship between the commercial entertainment they offered the public and the provision of alcohol. They were concerned from the start that, like gambling and game-fixing, alcohol could kill their enterprise. It would attract the wrong kind of customers. They also knew that in some cities the absence of alcohol would likely cost the business many patrons. Baseball addressed the same issues as America faced. Should it be "wet" or "dry?"

Alcohol was ubiquitous in nineteenth century America. New towns and old were filled with saloons. Many groceries and, later in the century, department stores, sold alcohol and little more. At times, making money was more important than being considered respectable. The evils of drink were well known, as was its temptation. Even at its inception in the 1840s, amateur baseball seemed simply a good excuse for a lavish dinner and the copious drink to follow the contest.

Colonial Americans drank considerable quantities of alcohol, perhaps three times as much as modern Americans. A diary kept aboard the Mayflower noted that the Pilgrims landed earlier than planned, "our victuals being much spent, especially our beer." Rightfully concerned about the purity of their water or milk, colonists found alcohol a safe substitute if consumed in moderation and at home, as it generally was. They enjoyed a daily portion of hard cider and whiskey. History records little concern about colonial drinking, although Virginia in 1671 did attempt to stop drunkenness. For the most part overuse was socially controlled, and it rarely contaminated the public spaces. Puritans even called alcohol the "Good Creature of God."

In the decades that followed independence, misbehavior occasioned by excessive consumption of alcohol in public became the object of public regulation. Far ahead of his time, Dr. Benjamin Rush, a signer of the Declaration of Independence, suggested that alcohol abuse was a disease. Those who were "drunkards," the term then in common use, should receive medical treatment, and they should not be punished. The only cure available was total abstinence. And the only way one could stay clear of the seduction of spirits was through religious devotion.

In the nineteenth century, as America mechanized and then industrialized, drink became an object of solace for many workers rather than a mere accompaniment for social interaction. As members of the middle and upper classes decreased their consumption, alcohol misuse became a badge of the lower classes. During the middle decades of the nineteenth century, waves of European immigrants brought their drinking habits with them to America. German immigrants, including Miller, Schlitz, Anheuser and Busch, brought their families and their recipes for beer to America. Irish immigrants, escaping from the famine in their homeland, came to America in the 1850s and brought with them a taste for hard liquor.

Alcohol use in the nineteenth century reflected the three major strains of the changing American landscape — immigration, religious fervor and the dramatic social dislocation brought about by reformed work patterns. Proper society associated their fear of immigrants with the overuse of alcohol. Nativist sentiment focused on the immigrants' "demon rum" and high-potency beer. Alcohol came to be seen in Calvinist America as an "attractive vice" and a significant source of societal dysfunction. As mechanization and industrialization offered workers some leisure time, those with any income were likely to drink away their earnings.

The temperance movement in America formally began in 1826 with the establishment of the American Temperance Society. Millions took the pledge not to imbibe, and the daily press joined the temperance chorus. In 1852, the *New York Times* railed against the 500–600 "grog shops and bar-rooms" which, in violation of the law, were open in the City on the Sabbath: "These nurseries of dissipation, licentiousness and crime thrive even more prosperously on Sunday then during the rest of the week." A saloon was a den of iniquity, "too unrespectable to tolerate." If it was closed on Sunday, the "weak-minded," who labored the other six days, "would be saved." As it was, especially on Third Avenue, "horse-racing, fighting, drinking, and insulting peaceably-disposed citizens are the order of the day." The "three-penny poison" raised serious questions as to state of the democracy, according to the *Times*.

On the other hand, the immigrant community viewed all prohibitionists as nativists in church clothing. They sternly rejected being "uplifted" by Protestant fanatics. The debate mirrored the ethnic and religious fault lines of a changing America. Resisting forced socialization and assimilation, European immigrant groups saw alcohol consumption in a social setting as a matter of personal liberty. Wasn't that what America was about?

A mass meeting of thousands of immigrants in New York in 1855 heard from ex-alderman (and not yet Boss) Tweed and other spokesmen appealing to the new American crowd. They denounced the effort to ban sale of alcoholic beverages as "tyrannical." Men had a "natural right" to drink as they pleased. They likened prohibition to enforced prayer and compelled haircuts. "Abstract morality urged on by fanatical zeal would do great injury to humanity."

Saloons played a critical social role in American life. In a saloon, Charles Loring Brace wrote, a man "can find jolly companions, a lighted and warmed room, a newspaper, and, above all, a draught which can change poverty into riches, and drive care and labor and the thought of all his burdens and annoyances far away." At stake in the prohibition battle was both personal self-esteem in a harsh world and a way of life for new arrivals on these shores. This public and political war over alcohol, sin and tyranny would rage for the next 65 years until the Prohibitionists ultimately prevailed through the enactment of a constitutional amendment.

On the eve of the Civil War, a census showed that there was one saloon in New York City for every fifteen families. Only one percent of the established saloons carried the required city license. In addition to "tippling," these establishments also offered "dance, comic songs, concerts, billiards and roulette tables." The results of these temptations were apparent: "[I]t is wasteful of money and health, it engenders pauperism, it causes crime, promotes lawlessness, and it tends to irreligion and infidelity." New York's Sabbath Committee proposed a series of interesting "remedies," including a change in payday to Monday or Wednesday, the provision of alternative "innocent and healthful popular recreation," and the "establishment of public fountains, where laborers could slake their thirst [on water] without being driven to the dram-shop."

After the Civil War, the nation's "gross wickedness" of spirits continued unabated. Dominant social and economic groups intensified their battle over alcohol consumption. The Women's Christian Temperance Union, formed in Indianapolis on March 3, 1874, led the charge against this "socially and morally deviant" behavior. The National Anti-Saloon League joined the battle in 1895, focusing first on the sale of intoxicated beverages to minors. This "red-hot fight," the *Washington Post* reported on April 16, 1895, "would meet with the heartfelt approval of citizens and generally win the league the recognition to which its numbers entitle it."

The battle against demon rum was rooted deeply in the nation's religiosity. America had always been a Protestant nation. Contrary to popular myth, religious dissenters in America were always shunned, avoided, and, at times, persecuted. The First Amendment to the Constitution only assured the various Protestant sects that one denomination would not be made officially predominant over the others, but no one thought that Catholics, Jews and others would be able to ascend to societal and political acceptability, let alone prominence. Intolerance of religious differences has been the norm throughout the nation's history.

Protestant ministers used their pulpits to scold those groups, normally Catholics, who would not take the pledge against alcohol use. Temperance and the religious revival spurred public action. The *Chicago Tribune* reported on February 21, 1899, that 250 ministers from Presbyterian, Baptist, Congregational and Methodist denominations had joined forces in this battle for prohibition. That summer, Reverend J. Q. A. Henry told his Chicago congregants: "The twentieth century will see the triumph either of the Christian church or of the saloon."

Employers in the Gilded Age railed against the evils of alcoholism and its disruptive influence on employee attendance and performance in the workplace. An employee who engaged in drunkenness and its "natural consequence," debauchery, in his off-duty hours could not be counted on to fulfill the obligations of his job. Alcoholism plagued employers and employees alike, and liquor was everywhere.

The ultimate success of the movement, national Prohibition through the Eighteenth Amendment to the Constitution, would not be achieved until 1920. In the interim, those who sought to cleanse society of the cursed drink would be challenged by those public persons who freely imbibed, like the beloved Civil War hero Ulysses Grant, folklorist Mark Twain and, as we shall see, many baseball players and fans.

Evangelist Billy Sunday, a major league ballplayer during the nineteenth century who drank his share during his nine-year career on the diamond, achieved national prominence for his "dry" oratory and inspired preaching. Sunday liked to recall the exact moment when he found his true calling. He was sitting with friends on a street corner in Chicago "tanked up" when he heard a gospel troop singing hymns across the way. Sunday began to cry, remembering his religious childhood. He crossed the road bidding farewell to his pals: "Goodbye boys. I'm through. I'm going to Jesus. We have come to a parting of the ways." (Actually, he continued to play baseball for a few years, but never on Sundays.)

As a preacher, Rev. Sunday used baseball metaphors to great advantage: the religious should throw "a fastball at the devil;" sinners will be "dying on second or third base." In Detroit in the fall of 1916, Sunday ignited the crowd with his "muscularity" and his abundant adjectives, attacking the

> hog-jowled, weasel-eyed, sponge-columned, mushy-fisted, jelly-spined, pussy-footing, four-flushing, charlotte russe Christians.

Lord save us from off-handed, flabby-cheeked, brittle-boned, weak-kneed, thin-skinned, pliable, plastic, spineless, effeminate, ossified, three-karat Christianity.... Help me, Jesus, to lasso and corral the young man on his way to hell. Help me save the young girl merchandising her womanhood. Help me, Jesus, help me save all in Detroit who are rushing to hell so fast that you can't see them for the dust.

On the eve of Prohibition and ultimate victory, Reverend Sunday regaled a huge crowd and a radio audience:

The reign of tears is over. The slums will soon be a memory. We will turn our prisons into factories and our jails into storehouses and corncribs. Men will walk upright now, women will smile and the children will laugh. Hell will forever be rent.

That did not happen, of course, although during the thirteen years of Prohibition there was a reduction in alcohol-related diseases. It did result in shutting saloons, but liquor was easily available for those with money. Fundamental habits do not change easily in a consumer society.

Prohibition did not outlaw drinking alcohol. It only prohibited "the manufacture, sale or transportation of intoxicating liquors." (Even so, during Prohibition, minor league ballplayers in the Quebec-Ontario-Vermont League smuggled spirits across the border into the United States.) Federal prohibition of alcohol was built on a weak political consensus, and the clash of cultures evidenced over a century of struggle doomed the national interdiction and led to its repeal in 1933 with the enactment of the Twenty-First Amendment to the Constitution.

Baseball and Alcohol

Spectators at early baseball games were not separated from the field of play. Lubricated by hard liquor, onlookers would run on to the field to object to an umpire's call. Some would even grab a bat and seek to aid their favored club by participating in the game when the need arose.

The National League decided at its formation in 1876 to ban the sale of alcohol at all baseball grounds, and promised a "new and very severe penalty for drunkenness." It also banned play on Sunday as an appeal to the religious sensibilities of America. Some states and cities had enacted Blue Laws as early as the eighteenth century to preserve tranquility on the Lord's Day. The League's Sunday ban also had the benefit of excluding most lower-class laborers from the ballparks, because they only could attend on Sunday, their one day off from work. The *Chicago Tribune* had explained in 1880 the true benefits of eliminating "beer-jerking" and Sunday play. Games on the Sabbath were contrary to "sound business policy":

> [Baseball] is supported by a class of people by whom these practices are regarded as an abomination — a class of people whose patronage is of infinite greater value in dollars and cents, let along respectability, than that of the element of people for whom beer is an attraction and a necessity.

The Sunday prohibition lasted well into the twentieth century in many major league cities. Philadelphia became the last city to allow Sunday baseball, in 1934.

The National League owners voted in 1878 to expel from the new league any club that sold beer. The resolution was directed at the Cincinnati franchise, which ignored the edict, sold beer and rented its field for Sunday play. When that club refused to sign the "no-beer" pledge, the owners dropped it from the League in 1881.

A rival circuit, the American Association, formed late in 1881, was scorned by National League magnates as the "Beer and Whiskey League." The Association fielded six clubs, including the exiled Cincinnati Red Stockings club that won the first Association pennant in 1882. The Association sought out a working class audience, allowing both the sale of alcohol and Sunday play — all at half the price charged by the National League.

It was no coincidence that four American Association club owners owned breweries. Chris Von der Ahe, the exuberant German-born

"Millionaire Sportsman" who owned the St. Louis Brown Stockings, knew nothing about the game of baseball. He did appreciate that baseball would be profitable for his saloon and grocery store that were located near the baseball grounds. He bought Sportsman's Park and later added a covered grandstand and long bar for the sale of beer. He then introduced sausages to go with the beer, creating, some say, the link between baseball and hot dogs. A large man with a bulbous nose and notable moustache, Von der Ahe would become one of the game's great promoters. He was the first to refer to his customers as "fanatics," later shortened by sportswriters to "fans," although there is some dispute that this is the origin of the word. (Spectators at the time were more likely referred to as "cranks.") When the American Association folded in 1891, Von der Ahe bought the National League franchise in St. Louis, adding a dance hall to Sportsman's Park and amusement park rides in center field, a racetrack and an all-female cornet band. Later he promoted attendance at the "Coney Island of the West" by offering a double-header for four bits: a game of baseball followed by Buffalo Bill's Wild West Show. On the second day of the 1898 season, Sportsman's Park burned to the ground in a half hour, and Von der Ahe went bankrupt.

The National League's magnates continued to present an image of propriety in appealing to its target audience. In 1882, the league blacklisted players for "gross acts of insubordination or intemperance." Through the decade of the 1880s, the owners gave the league president unprecedented power to discipline players, managers and umpires for being drunk or fighting in public. The league president could fine, suspend or blacklist any participant who "in any manner brought disgrace upon the profession of base ball playing by his open conduct."

That did not stop players from drinking. They continued to pursue libation before and after the games, both in and away from the ballpark. Perhaps the greatest power hitter of his day, right fielder Ed Delahanty, was often drunk on and off the field, and, as a result, his behavior was constantly "pugnacious and obstreperous." He bet heavily on the horses and lost. The best of the five Delahanty brothers who played major league ball in the nineteenth century, his ability to play the game made him a hero to many. On July 13, 1896, Delahanty hit four consecutive inside-the-park home runs (and a single to boot), but alcohol would finally do him in.

In his sixteenth and last year in the major leagues, Delahanty continued to hit with authority for the Washington Senators of the new American League, although he was overweight and sluggish in the field. His club suspended him from play after he missed a game in Cleveland because he was drunk. Despondent, Delahanty traveled east on the Michigan Central No. 6 from Detroit to New York City, drinking the whole way. After he threatened fellow passengers with a straight razor, John Cole, the train conductor, put him off the train at Bridgeburg on the Canadian side of the Niagara River right on the International Bridge. Within an hour, he would be dead. After a confrontation with a night watchman, Delahanty staggered along the railroad tracks in the dark chasing the train, fell through an open drawbridge and was swept over Niagara Falls to his death. Searchers found the mangled body of the 35-year-old a week later. In 1945, the veteran committee voted Delahanty into the Hall of Fame.

The 1885 *Spalding Guide* blamed the widespread alcohol use on the players' new-found riches:

> The rapid increase in the compensation of ball players soon opened up another avenue of trouble for the League, which needed and received prompt attention. This was flagrant and open dissipation in the ranks at home and abroad. While this was confined comparatively to a few men, the innocent suffered largely from it, and the National League was brought into disrepute. Heroic measures were again adopted, and several players were indefinitely suspended, with excellent effect.

Apparently, the "heroic measures" adopted were to cut player salaries. The Guide promoted total abstinence, but such an island of temperance could never exist in an urban culture where alcohol was a quintessential part of daily social life.

Concerned about excessive alcohol use by ballplayers, baseball clubs hired detectives to follow their charges and catch them in the "great elbow act" at the bar. The going rate to hire these Pinkerton men was five dollars a day for "shadowing" and six dollars for "investigating." The rather-obvious Pinkertons often ended up on the short end of saloon brawls. The practice of management hiring private detectives to spy on baseball players continued well into the twentieth century.

Using the alternative strategy of positive reinforcement, some owners offered players bonuses for good behavior. In the 1880s, the Cincinnati club gave its catcher Kid Baldwin forty dollars for his exemplary conduct, although his work on the field was hardly noteworthy. Although short-lived, the league's Brush Classification Plan of 1888 ranked a player's salary in part based on his "habits, earnestness and special qualifications." Sobriety was given a monetary value.

Players who could not break their alcohol addiction and disruptive behavior might be banned for life by the league. Longtime Pittsburgh Pirates owner Barney Dreyfuss in 1911 included a provision in every one of his players' contracts that mandated abstinence from alcohol. Pittsburgh's Hall of Fame manager Fred Clarke rarely enforced it.

The Scourge of Alcoholism

The use of alcohol was widespread among baseball players, an integral part of the culture of baseball, but that did not mean that drinking was always a matter of choice. Some of the game's greatest players, such as "Old Pete" Grover Cleveland Alexander, were afflicted with alcoholism. Alexander, it was said, was drunk when he pitched against the Yankees in the 1926 World Series. His affliction was as widely known as his talent, although a long article extolling his virtues in The *Baseball Magazine* in 1916 stated: "It goes without saying that Alexander is free from the vice of drink, which has cursed many a ball player's career." Alexander's managers knew better. They were alternately tolerant or disgusted by his behavior, but Alexander could not beat his illness. Cardinals manager Rogers Hornsby later remarked: "I would rather have him pitch a crucial game for me drunk, than anyone I've ever known sober. He was that good." Alexander told sportswriter Fred Lieb: "Sure I tried to stop — I just couldn't."

Throughout his life, Chicago magnate Albert Spalding championed temperance among professional ballplayers. As a former major league pitcher himself, Spalding could preach from the pulpit of experience. Yet his puritanical views fell on deaf ears. Drinking was "immoral," he proclaimed, as if that would end the practice among those who were addicted. His views, he claimed, were simply a reaction to the public's concern about the "dissipation of some of the players." Spalding hired Pinkerton detectives to spy on the fifteen players on his team as they caroused through the Tenderloin district of Chicago. As he wrote in his autobiography, "The report showed that the records of seven of the fifteen players were too colorful for patient consideration." He read the report aloud to his players, and star player Mike "King" Kelly objected: "I've only got this to say. When the detective says I had a lemonade at three o-clock in the morning, he's off. It was straight whiskey. Mike Kelly never drank a lemonade in his life." For a while, the players listened to Spalding's orders that they behave. A week later, however, after they dropped games in Boston, Kelly explained to the press that the team performance was the result of "too much temperance."

After they were involved in fights with the Pinkertons, Spalding sold the contracts of boozing Chicago stars Mike Kelly and Jim McCormick, both of whom regularly "bowled up" on whiskey before a game, to other clubs. These "sensational" transactions, as the newspapers called them in 1887, were "for their own good as well as our own," claimed Spalding, who pocketed thousands of dollars. Spalding sold Kelly to Boston for $10,000. The most popular ballplayer of his era, he became a great fan favorite among the Irish of Boston and attendance soared at Beaneater contests. A marvelous base runner, he is credited with developing the hook slide and inspiring the hit 1893 song "Slide, Kelly, Slide." Toward the end of his career, he opened a saloon in New York, not the best post-career placement for an alcoholic. (The 1893 *Spalding Baseball Guide* reported that eighty percent of all ball players who went into business after leaving the game invested in saloons "with a belief that their supposed great popularity will draw them a fortune-making patron-age.") Kelly's performance on the field rapidly deteriorated over his four seasons in Boston, and by 1894 he was back in the minor leagues. That fall he developed pneumonia, and he whispered as he was carried through the hospital door, "This is my last slide." On November 8, 1894, he died penniless and alone at the age of 36.

Spalding dealt McCormick to the Pittsburgh Alleghenys, where he played in 1887 on the club with star hurler Jimmy Galvin. In his prime, McCormick had been known for his "raise ball," but alcohol had taken its toll. McCormick led the Pittsburgh club in hit batsmen, wild pitches, walks and losses. It was his tenth and final season in the major leagues.

For those players he could not trade, Spalding used the stick. He drafted appropriate language to place in the standard player contract all professional players were required to sign:

> As an inducement to every player to so regulate his habits and ac-tions as to keep at all times in a sound and healthy condition, the League contract provides that there shall be no wages paid where no services are rendered; that for the period during which a player is suspended or excused from play, for any of the above men-tioned reasons, he shall forfeit such a ratable proportion of his wages, for the season, as the number of games not played by him bears to the total number of games scheduled for the season.

To deal with the alcoholism of his veteran pitcher Ray "Slim" Cald-well, Cleveland Indians manager Tris Speaker adopted a unique ap-proach. In 1920, Speaker required Caldwell to follow the following regimen:

> After each game he pitches, Ray Caldwell must get drunk. He is not to report to the clubhouse the next day. The second day he is to report to Manager Speaker and run around the ballpark as many times as Manager Speaker stipulates. The third day he is to pitch batting practice, and the fourth day he is to pitch in a cham-pionship game.

That year, at age 38 Caldwell went 20–10 and pitched (but lost) a game for the World Champion Indians in their four-games-to-three Series victory over the Brooklyn Robins. Caldwell only lasted one more year in the majors, but pitched for another decade in the minor leagues.

Philadelphia Athletics pitcher Rube Waddell and his catcher Ossee Schreckengost were both alcoholics. They roomed together from 1902–1907. Waddell's contract with Philadelphia contained a provision that prohibited him from eating crackers in bed. Schrecongost insisted on this provision. In those days, players shared a double bed on the road.

Waddell tended bar when he was not drinking at one. His favorite was Brogan's, in Philadelphia. Later in his career with the St. Louis Browns, management attempted to keep Waddell out of trouble by employing him in the off season as a hunter. It worked, albeit briefly. Rube's drinking continued, and it took its toll. As he was failing, he wrote an open letter to young ballplayers: "Tell the boys to keep away from booze and cigarettes. I had my chance, and a good one it was. Many of the boys may have a better one ahead of them than I had. If they will leave the booze alone, they won't have any trouble."

It was also not uncommon for Schreckengost to miss a game because of his alcohol problem. First baseman Harry Davis convinced manager and owner Connie Mack to keep "Schreck" (as he was known) on the club if he switched to milk shakes, some 15–20 a day. At times, Davis accompanied Schreck to the drugstore to make sure he was complying with Mack's directive. Once Davis went to the drugstore alone and asked for a shake like Schreck would order. The clerk reached under the counter and filed Davis's glass half with milk and half with sherry.

Waddell and Schreckengost died within a few months of each other in 1914. Waddell died of tuberculosis in April of that year at age 37. Schreck was distraught over the passing of his long-time battery mate. He told his friends that he "did not care to live now. The 'Rube' is gone, and I am all in. I might as well join him." He collapsed in a Philadelphia café, and died in Northwestern General Hospital a few days later at age 39 "from a complication of diseases."

Although always ready to criticize their employees for their dissipation, the owners did not themselves abstain from alcohol. The *Sporting News* reported that the real business among the club owners always took place at a bar. Even baseball's National Commission in the early twentieth century did most of its work in the rathskeller of the Hotel Sinton in Cincinnati.

Baseball management often criticized players for alcohol abuse, but it rarely did anything to help players confront their dependency. The Chicago White Stockings did visit Hot Springs, Arkansas in the spring of 1886 to "boil out the alcoholic microbes," but there is no indication it worked. Babe Ruth also visited the spa in the 1920s, but that certainly failed to arrest his excessive drinking. Don Newcombe, the Dodger pitcher, acknowledged that alcohol abuse shortened his career:

> There is a distinct lack of concern on the part of management. It's paranoia on their part. They want to keep it quiet and out of the newspapers. They want you to believe that nothing like this could happen in their organization.

Even with rehabilitation, alcoholism is a tough customer. Dodger and Yankee pitcher Steve Howe was suspended numerous times and repeatedly sought drug and alcohol rehabilitation, but to no avail. He could not break his addiction.

Throughout the history of the game, many ballplayers battled alcohol and lost. A few stand out as particularly notorious. Curt Welch, centerfielder for the St. Louis Browns from 1885–1887, hid a pint of whiskey in the outfield grass at Sportsman's Park. He would take nips between batters. Pete Browning, the "Gladiator," was normally drunk on and off the field. Nonetheless, he batted .341 for his career, the twelfth highest all-time major league batting average. Browning, who played right field for Louisville in the American Association, said "I can't hit the ball until I hit the bottle." Browning once got left behind in St. Louis in 1887 because he was too drunk to find the train. There is a story about a drunk Browning taking a 15-foot lead off second base in 1887 and then falling asleep. The second baseman "walked up and put him out, to the intense

Pete Browning, the "Gladiator," was normally drunk on and off the field. A lifetime .341 hitter, Browning said "I can't hit the ball until I hit the bottle."

disgust of the spectators." Even with his substance abuse (or perhaps because of it), Browning was either first, second or third in the league in hitting from 1882–1891. Returning home to Louisville after finishing his career, Browning operated a saloon, then sold cigars and eventually, as a result of extensive brain damage from his heavy drinking, was declared insane. He died shortly thereafter.

The twentieth century had its share of serious alcoholics. The *Cleveland Plain Dealer* reported in 1997 that "Sudden Sam" McDowell, Cleveland's great pitcher in the 1960s, "said he could throw a martini olive through a concrete wall if he hadn't been so fond of drinking the cocktail first." For baseball fans who grew up in the New York metropolitan area in the 1950s, Mickey Mantle offered a role model of courage in the face of great physical pain. His Hall of Fame performance as the Yankees centerfielder inspired a generation of youngsters. We did not know, of course, how much alcohol Mick had consumed in the process. When he received a liver transplant in 1994, Mantle told America about his alcoholism and urged youngsters not to follow his example. Finally, he sought treatment at the Betty Ford Clinic, but it was too late to reverse a lifetime of physical and emotional damage.

Nineteenth Century Drug Abuse

In the 1870s, Tommy Barlow played four years of baseball in the National Association, the predecessor to the National League. He is credited with inventing the bunt hit using a 24-inch bat. He was also a dope addict. Catching for the Hartford Dark Blues, he was the backstop for William Charles "Cherokee" Fisher, considered a "lightning pitcher." Hit in the ribs by one of Fisher's offerings, Barlow was transported to his hotel where a doctor administered morphine for the pain. Barlow became hooked on the drug.

The first great American epidemic in drug use was the result of the Civil War. Some 300,000 soldiers came home from the Civil War with a dependency to morphine, the so-called "army disease." Tommy Barlow was just one of its later casualties.

It is estimated that during the nineteenth century some 5 percent of the American public was addicted to opium and its derivatives. By mid-century, opium was sold legally across the country, and it was easily available. Some extolled the virtues of the drug. The *Daily Graphic* reported about an exotic New York City opium den:

> Those in the habit of coming here say that it has a beneficial medicinal effect, and, if only inhaled in small quantities, animates the spirits and gives energy to the intellectual powers, at the same time imparting a languor to the body, leaving the mind free from nervous effects.

By the mid-nineteenth century, Friedrich Gaedcke, a German chemist, had extracted cocaine from the South American coca leaf, and the German army used this new substance to keep its Bavarian troops alert. In 1863, Angelo Mariani, an Italian pharmacist, created a cocaine-and-wine drink called "Vin Mariani" that was a worldwide sensation. Even Pope Leo XIII enjoyed the new libation and bestowed upon the discoverer a gold medal. Vin Mariani won a medal at a London exhibition and was declared the "wine of athletes." It was available at retail in Los Angeles in 1890 for 94 cents a bottle or by mail order in Atlanta for a few pennies more. Vin Mariani was widely advertised well into the twentieth century.

American surgeon William Halsted, a founder of Johns Hopkins School of Medicine, used a four-percent solution of cocaine as an anesthetic, and he became addicted to the substance himself, along with many other physicians and dentists. The *American Magazine* in 1885 regaled cocaine's "practical importance" and "great value." In 1895, Heinrich Dreser, working for the Bayer Company of Elberfeld, Germany, diluted morphine with acetyls to produce a substance without the common morphine side effects. Bayer produced and marketed diacetylmorphine under the brand name "heroin."

Patent medicines, such as Hunt's Lightning Oil, Ayer's Cherry Pectoral, Darby's Carminative, Godfrey's Cordial, McMunn's Elixir of Opium, Dover's Powder, Wintersmith's Chill Tonic, Gooch's Mexican Syrup, and Mrs. Winslow's Soothing Syrup, made abundant use of the active ingredient morphine. Parke-Davis included cocaine in 15 different products, and sold it in pure form with a syringe. Its advertisements boasted that cocaine "could make the coward brave, the silent eloquent, and render the sufferer insensitive to pain." In 1886, an Atlanta pharmacist, John Pemberton, added cocaine to a soft drink using kola nuts and concocted Coca-Cola. The liquid refreshment later removed this secret ingredient.

Users could obtain opiates over the counter in pharmacies, from their physicians, at grocery stories, or by mail order. Salesmen delivered cocaine door-to-door. Opium poppies were grown legally across America. Congress banned opium in 1905, but did not outlaw heroin until 1924 after intensive lobbying by the tobacco interests.

Amphetamines

When Jim Bouton published his book *Ball Four* in 1970, the reaction of the American public was as remarkable as Bouton's revelations. Could his stories of amphetamine "greenies" in the locker room be true? There was general disbelief followed by anger. According to Bouton, "greenies" were an essential part of a ballplayer's preparation for the daily game and "a lot of baseball players couldn't function without them." The little pills — also variously called "uppers" or "speed"— worked effectively to stimulate a user's central nervous system, and they became a regular part of many baseball players' pre-game preparation.

Could ballplayers possibly drink as much alcohol as Bouton claimed? The drink of choice was beer and the consumption was certainly copious. Anyone who had followed the sport, of course, knew about these addictions and the other dysfunctional pastimes of the players. Bouton's book was no surprise to anyone who had been paying attention. It also did not endear him to his former teammates. Howard Cosell put it bluntly: "That kid must have a death wish." Joe Garagiola said that Bouton made him feel like he needs a shower. When asked what he thought of Bouton's book, Mickey Mantle responded: "Jim who?"

The portrait Bouton painted of modern baseball players was not pretty. In addition to pep pills and alcohol consumption, players would cheat on their wives, play games while hungover, fight on the team bus, and racially taunt their teammates and opponents. It was a vulgar and disgusting portrait of the heroes of the National Game. Bouton's book was discordant with the prevailing "gee whiz" genre of baseball autobiographies, such as Christy Mathewson's *Pitching in a Pinch* in 1912 and Joe DiMaggio's *Lucky to Be a Yankee* in 1946. DiMaggio had dedicated his book to "all the ballplayers in both leagues, a clean bunch of fellows and all grand sports."

After the publication of Bouton's expose, Baseball Commissioner Bowie Kuhn summoned Bouton to New York from Houston where he was pitching for the Astros. He publicly castigated Bouton for his book and warned him not to do it again: "I advised Mr. Bouton of my displeasure with these writings." Bouton was unrepentant: "I still am glad I wrote the book. I had something to say and I won't apologize for any of it." He also added that he hoped the Commissioner's scolding would help sales.

Amphetamines had first been synthesized by a Romanian chemist named Lazar Edeleano in 1887, and they were marketed over-the-counter in inhaler form in the 1930s to treat congestion. Athletes first used the new substance about that time as a performance stimulant replacing strychnine. During the Second World War and the Vietnam War, American troops used amphetamines to stay awake on the battlefield. It was not until the Drug Abuse Regulation and Control Act of 1970 that their sale without a prescription was regulated by law. Amphetamines are sympathomimetic amines like ephedrine that chemically activate nerve cells in the brain and spinal cord. This, in turn, increases a user's alertness and lessens his fatigue. There are several common side effects, such as change in mood, insomnia, and restlessness. As a Schedule II controlled substance, amphetamines are available only by prescription, but they have been extensively abused throughout society and not just by ballplayers.

Although it was hard for anyone to be greatly surprised after Bouton's revelations, there was some astonishment when, on September 13, 1985, it was reported that John Milner had testified before the grand jury in the Pittsburgh cocaine trafficking trials that the great Willie Mays kept a bottle of "red juice"— liquid amphetamine — in his locker during his final season with the Mets in 1973:

> Milner: "Willie had the red juice."
> Q: "Willie who?"
> A: "Mays."
> Q: "Willie Mays?"
> A: "That's right, the great one, yes."

"I tried it once," Milner said. "I don't know what kind of speed it was, but it kept your eyes open." Mays later responded that he did not recall having anything in his locker like that.

Ballplayers and Recreational Drugs

Modern ballplayers have also struggled with the use of, and addiction to, so-called "recreational drugs." Pirates pitcher Dock Ellis claimed he pitched his June 12, 1970 no-hitter against the Padres while under the influence of LSD. He could only remember bits and pieces of the game:

I was psyched. I had a feeling of euphoria. I was zeroed in on the [catcher's] glove, but I didn't hit the glove too much. I remember hitting a couple of batters and the bases were loaded two or three times. The ball was small sometimes, the ball was large sometimes. Sometimes I saw the catcher, sometimes I didn't. Sometimes I tried to stare the hitter down and throw while I was looking at him. I chewed my gum until it turned to powder. They say I had about three to four fielding chances. I remember diving out of the way of a ball I thought was a line drive. I jumped, but the ball wasn't hit hard and never reached me.

An alcoholic and drug abuser, Ellis left the game in 1979 to pursue treatment. He later worked as a rehabilitation consultant for criminal convicts.

Recreational drugs, like cocaine and marijuana, have been the bane of numerous baseball superstars. Dwight Gooden, Vida Blue, and Darryl Strawberry made headlines for taking these drugs. Montreal's great base stealer, Tim Raines, admitted that he would slide headfirst into second base to protect the cocaine he kept in his back pocket. He had a $1000-a-week habit while he played the game. In 1982, he entered a San Diego clinic for treatment, returned to the game and played for twenty more years.

The criminal drugs trials in Pittsburgh in 1985 uncovered the

Pirates pitcher Dock Ellis claimed he pitched his June 12, 1970 no-hitter against the Padres while under the influence of LSD.

extent of the use of recreational drugs by ballplayers, focusing particularly on cocaine. Although no players were indicted, testimony revealed that Keith Hernandez and other players had used illegal substances. Baseball Commissioner Peter Ueberroth imposed serious penalties on seven ballplayers, who were suspended for a year, and lesser penalties on a dozen additional players. Afterwards, Ueberroth announced that "baseball's drug problem is over." Despite his authoritative pronouncement, baseball continued to be plagued by recreational drug use throughout the following decades.

The Steroid Scandal

The Major League Baseball's steroid scandal of the twenty-first century has focused the public's attention once again on the use of performance-enhancing substances in the National Game. All players know that run production translates into salary production. As Ralph Kiner said: "Home runs hitters drive Cadillacs; singles hitters drive Fords." Although only a few players were involved with steroids, when Congressional hearings spotlighted some of the sport's greatest stars, it convinced many Americans that the game was not on the level. The facts notwithstanding, baseball came in for another scolding.

In 1994, 1,084,000 Americans, or 0.5 percent of the adult population, said that they had used anabolic steroids, according to the Substance Abuse and Mental Health Services Administration's National Household Survey on Drug Abuse. In the 18–34 age group, about 1 percent of the young men had used steroids, about the same percentage of major league ballplayers of the same age who tested positive for steroid use.

Only two major league players have admitted using steroids. Jose Canseco told us that "steroids is the future." It was certainly his past. He claimed he used steroids starting in 1984 until he left the game in 2001. As the self-proclaimed "godfather of steroids," Canseco had no regrets. Another user did have regrets. The National League's Most Valuable Player in 1996, Ken Caminiti, admitted in 2002 that he had used steroids during that great season when he hit .326 with 40 home runs and 130 runs batted in. Caminiti was also an alcoholic and a drug addict. Eight days after he was released by the Braves in 2001 he was arrested in a Houston crack house. Caminiti died of a heart attack after a drug overdose in October 2004 at age 41 in a hospital in the Bronx.

On November 15, 2007, the United States Attorney in San Francisco announced that the grand jury investigating the BALCO affair had returned an indictment against Barry Bonds, alleging that he had committed perjury in his testimony before the grand jury regarding his use of steroids. Months earlier Bonds had set a new career record for home runs, aided, many thought, by performance enhancing drugs. For many in the media who had covered the accusations against Bonds, this was final proof of his mendacity. Only time — and the due process of a criminal trial — will tell us whether the accusations are true beyond a reasonable doubt.

The public contretemps about the comparatively minor use of steroids finally compelled owners and players to revise their drug testing scheme. Without any proof of the effect of steroid use on game performance or assurance as to the privacy of the results, the parties struggled to satisfy Congressional leaders, lest they lose credibility with the audience or be subjected to thoughtless oversight. Much as Commissioner Landis's draconian rule drove game-fixing (but not gambling) from baseball, the new testing plan drove steroids from the game. The only cost was to the privacy rights of the ballplayers.

Today, those fortunate athletes who rise to the major league level are exceedingly well compensated for their performance on the field. In exchange for their status we demand that they meet a high moral standard on and off the field and that they relinquish their privacy. Their predecessors carried this baggage of clean living with inconsistent success. Leo Durocher, no angel as a player or a manager, once said: "If any of my players don't take a drink now and then, they'll be gone. You don't play this game on gingersnaps."

The Babe, Matty
and the Iron Horse

Perhaps the foremost demonstration of dysfunctional living off the field by a baseball player was offered by George Herman "Babe" Ruth. No one can doubt his enormous impact on the game on the field, but off the field he represented all the excesses of the Roaring Twenties. As Burt Whitman, a Boston sportswriter, wrote in 1918 before Ruth's sale to the Yankees: "The more I see of Babe, the more he seems a figure out of mythology."

Babe Ruth enjoyed living on the edge. Babe drank whiskey for breakfast. In spring training with the Yankees in 1921, he was so drunk that he ran into a palm tree in the outfield and was knocked unconscious. Did his rambling life help his game? Sportswriter W. O. McGeehan wrote, referring to the Babe: "I am quite sure that statistics will show that the greatest number of successes have been scored by those who have led moderately dirty lives." There was nothing "moderate" about Babe's off-the-field antics, however.

The Babe had difficulty accepting any authority other than that offered by his own free will. After the 1921 season, Ruth and other World Series winning ballplayers barnstormed in violation of Commissioner Landis edict against such activity. He thought the Commissioner's rule was unfair, and so he did what he wanted, offering to Landis that he might "go jump in the lake." Landis did not take Ruth's advice: "It seems I'll have to show somebody who's running this game." The Commissioner suspended both Ruth and Yankee teammate Bob Meusel for the first 40 games of the 1922 season.

Not every ballplayer was an alcoholic or drug addict. Most were simply great athletes who entertained us over the decades. A few extraordinary baseball athletes deserved their Olympian status, thus proving to be the exceptions that made the rule. Giants pitcher Christy Mathewson was one such model. Grantland Rice said of Matty:

[He] brought something to baseball no one had ever given the game — not even Babe Ruth or Ty Cobb. He handed the game a certain touch of class, an indefinable life in culture, brains [and] personality.

In addition to his singular personal qualities, Matty won 373 games, the most in National League history. A college-educated player on a club where almost no other player had completed high school, Matty was a moral straight arrow who taught Sunday school and spoke to youth groups about clean living. As an officer during World War I, Matty suffered a poison gas attack and died prematurely from tuberculosis at age 45.

The "Iron Horse" Lou Gehrig is most remembered for his remarkable 2,130 continuous game streak, but he was also an exceptional role model for America's youth. On June 1, 1925, Gehrig entered a game as a pinch-hitter. Almost fourteen years later, on May 2, 1939, after Gehrig had been performing below his standard of true excellence and feeling quite weak, he benched himself. It was the last game he would play. As he stood at home plate in Yankee Stadium on July 4, 1939, he said, "For the past two weeks you have been reading about the bad break I got. Yet today, I consider myself the luckiest man on the face of the earth." America saw the genuine article, a hero among men who faced adversity with courage. His incurable condition, arterial lateral sclerosis, later became known as Lou Gehrig's disease. No one was perfect, but Gehrig was close.

The travails baseball players suffered from alcohol and drug abuse are sad tales of personal tragedy. As such, they present us with the genuine hardship that many endure each day, even without a golden glove or a steady bat. Americans confront alcohol and drug addiction in various ways, but normally out of the public spotlight. That does not relieve the misery. It only makes it private.

Hall-of-Famer Juan Marichal slammed his bat over the catcher's head three times while blood trickled from a two-inch gash above John Roseboro's left eye.

Chapter 5

Violence on the Field

"For all its gentility, its almost leisurely pace, baseball is violence under wraps."— Willie Mays

ON SUNDAY AFTERNOON, August 22, 1965, the Los Angeles Dodgers played their arch-rivals, the Giants, at the unfinished Candlestick Park in San Francisco before a sell-out crowd of 42,807, the best attendance of the season. The Giants trailed the Dodgers by a game in the National League standings and, by the third inning, were down 2–1 in the contest. It was a match-up between the two finest pitchers in the game, future Hall of Famers Sandy Koufax and Juan Marichal. In the top of the third inning, Marichal, the high-kicking Giants hurler who had won 19 games by late August, had thrown pitches at both Maury Wills and Ron Fairly aimed at their heads. Wills and Fairly had both gotten hits in their first at bats. Juan Marichal led off the bottom of the third inning for the home team. Dodgers catch John Roseboro had wanted Koufax to retaliate against Marichal, but he refused. Koufax's second pitch to Marichal was low and inside, driving him off the plate. When Roseboro threw the ball back to Koufax, he nicked Marichal's ear.

Marichal turned and screamed at the catcher: "Why do you do that? Why you do that?" Roseboro stood up, removed his mask, and starred straight at Marichal. Marichal snapped and did the unthinkable. He slammed his bat over the catcher's head three times while blood trickled from a two-inch gash above Roseboro's left eye. Koufax charged in from the mound, just missing the third swing from Marichal's bat. The benches emptied and the melee lasted fourteen minutes, one of major league baseball's nastiest brawls. The Giants glorious outfielder Willie Mays calmed the players on both teams and led Roseboro back to the Dodgers dugout, his cut and bloodied head covered with a towel. Mays sat with Roseboro for a few moments, near tears, sobbing "Johnny,

Johnny, I'm so sorry." The umpire tossed Marichal from the game. When order was restored, Koufax got two quick outs, then walked two Giants and Willie Mays put the home team ahead for good with a three-run homer. After the game, some sports writer suggested that Mays should receive the Nobel Peace Prize. "Naw," said Mays, "no prizes for me." In fact, Mays was named the Most Valuable Player in the National League that season.

After the game, Dodger players called for National League president Warren Giles to suspend the Giants' best pitcher for the rest of the season, which would have sidelined Marichal for the remainder of the pennant race. Instead, Giles fined Marichal $1,750 (at the time the highest fine ever meted out to a player) and suspended him for eight days. Marichal missed only one turn on the mound, but he was banned from pitching against the Dodgers in their next series. The Dodgers ultimately won the pennant by just two games over the Giants.

Roseboro sued Marichal for $110,000 and threatened to press criminal assault charges. They settled the litigation out of court seven years later. Marichal telephoned Roseboro seeking forgiveness. Roseboro agreed, and the two warriors made peace. Roseboro later campaigned successfully for Marichal's election to the Hall of Fame in 1983, his third year of eligibility. They became very good friends, attending Old Timers games together and golfing. Marichal offered a eulogy at Roseboro's funeral in 2002. They are forever linked in the violent history of major league baseball.

Tempers can certainly erupt on the field at any time, especially when there is much at stake. The real wonder is why we have not seen batters use the implement they carry more often — the lethal weapon just the right length and weight to inflict a mortal blow on an opponent. While fisticuffs have been a regular part of the game since its inception, few players have attacked their opponents with the readily available weaponry.

Marichal's attack on Roseboro was not unprecedented, however. The earliest bat attack dates from 1873, when the Brooklyn Atlantics' star player "Fighting Bob" Ferguson was called upon to umpire a game between the New York Mutuals and a club from Baltimore. Ferguson, one of early baseball's stellar performers, was generally valued as tough and fair, but he was also quick to anger. Responding to abuse and insults from the New York Mutuals catcher Nat Hicks, Ferguson picked up a bat and pounded Hicks, breaking his arm. The catcher was sidelined for the next two months, but refused to press criminal charges.

Ferguson later fought gamblers who infested the ball yards using the same weapon as he used on Hicks. Sam Crane tells this story in the *New York Sunday American* on December 23, 1911, about a game played in Brooklyn in the 1870s:

> Just before the game was started and when the gamblers were flashing their money in big rolls and shouting their odds the loudest, Ferguson, taking a bat in his hand, strode over to the part of the grounds where the gamblers were located and in the presence of thousands of spectators charged them with collusion with the players to have the game thrown, and threatened to chastise any one or all of them if they did not desist. The gamblers slunk away like whipped curs, while the other spectators cheered "Fighting Bob" to the echo.

The game's first switch-hitter, long-time team captain, and a stellar fielder in the bare-handed era before the use of gloves, the flamboyant Ferguson earned the unique nickname "Death to Flying Things" for his ability to catch fly balls. When Ferguson ended his playing career, he became an umpire full-time. As might be imagined, he was firm and fearless and accepted no trickery.

"Devoid of a Single Brutal Feature"

With unbounded confidence, Albert Spalding in his *Official Base Ball Guide* in 1896 was able to exonerate the National Pastime from any accusations that it might be a violent sport:

> The decade of the nineties in the American athletic arena, as well as in that of Great Britain, has seen an era of brutalizing in sports

entered upon, which, it is to be hoped, time will end in due course. It has already culminated, and a sensible reaction set in, in 1894. In this connection, and without enumerating the specially brutal sports still in vogue, it is timely to state that our national game, while at the same time fully developing every true manly qualification in the form of courage, endurance, pluck and nerve, which the best of manly sports requires, is entirely devoid of a single brutal feature.

Despite this benediction, violent incidents on major league fields between baseball players were widespread in the decade of the 1890s, much as they were in the decades before and throughout the century to follow. In fact, in 1894 the same publication that two years later would pronounce baseball as a pacific endeavor, Spalding's definitive *Guide*, had rued the "hoodlumism" that had taken hold in the game. In 1895, Spalding complained that rowdy ball playing had resulted in "a decided falling off in the attendance of the best class of patrons of the professional clubs." This hoodlumism included "blackguard language; low cunning tricks, unworthy of manly players; brutal assaults on umpire and players; that nuisance of our ball fields, 'kicking,' and the dishonorable methods comprised in the term 'dirty ball playing.'"

In 1898, in order to stem the fights and nasty language that Spalding had already proclaimed gone from the game, National League magnates approved a resolution offered by owner John T. Brush that imposed heavy fines and suspensions on offending parties. Oliver "Patsy" Tebeau, manager of the Cleveland Spiders and a recidivist when it came to foul language and hurled epithets, responded tongue in cheek to the Brush resolution: "I figured that the restriction would save me a heap of unnecessary conversation. I was led to believe the patrons wanted a change and were in favor of speechless ball, something after the fashion of a deaf mute reunion." In fact, Tebeau would argue every pitch, and inspired his charges to do the same. He responded to every loud-mouthed fan. He challenged his players: "If there's any one on this club who wants to fight, just write it out and mail the challenge to me." On occasion, Tebeau had also been on the receiving end of the mayhem. Three years earlier in the post-season Temple Cup series, the Orioles John Mc-Graw had crunched Patsy Tebeau in the face and split open his lip.

The exploits and contests of skills that made baseball an attractive diversion — one played with "plenty of ginger," to use the phrase common at the turn of the twentieth century — sometimes made it a frenzied and tempestuous affair. As one of the chief culprits in "kicking" at umpires' calls and provoking fisticuffs at the slightest provocation, the "hard-boiled" John McGraw was incorrigible: "Sportsmanship and easy-going methods are all right, but it is the prospect of a hot fight that brings out the crowds." McGraw was the chief proponent of the "aggressive policy" that pervaded the National Game in the 1890s when he played for the old Baltimore Orioles and led them to three National League pennants that decade. The *Washington Post* opined in 1894: "Little McGraw, the Orioles third baseman, is being roasted all over the country for his efforts at dirty ball-playing. He will keep up that business until the National League will have to fire him out of the business." McGraw would stay in the business of baseball as a player and a very successful manager for the next forty years. He would later admit in *Liberty* magazine after his retirement that he had never acted out of anger: It was all "pure showmanship, deliberately planned."

"He was a scrappy ballplayer," Fred Lieb wrote about McGraw in 1912 in the *Baseball Magazine*, and he became a "scrappy manager.... Perhaps a little too scrappy, but a scrappy team generally draws well around the circuit." His actions — Lieb acknowledged that on a few occasions McGraw had "misbehaved on the field of battle"— demonstrated a propensity for violence. Join "ginger" with talent, and you have success. McGraw later explained that his rowdyism was designed to "change the entire aspect of a ball game and arouse the flagging spirits of my players." When disputes arose, McGraw resolved them with his fists. After a game in Cincinnati on June 8, 1917, from which McGraw had been ejected in the fifth inning, he brawled with the umpire who had insulted him, decking him with a right cross to the jaw. National League President John Tener fined him $500 and suspended him for 16 days. Although McGraw was not alone in taking "the battle" to the ballfield, he was its foremost proponent.

Although they regularly rued violence, club owners fully appreciated the attractiveness of an intense entertainment product with the ready potential for unrest. "Gunpowder for Breakfast!" That was what the owners advertised: "That's what the men on this base ball nine eat!" As journeyman major league manager Jack McKeon explained: "People come out to enjoy the game, but they want a little pepper in their soup." Humorist Art Buchwald, writing only half in jest in 1983, suggested that: "Baseball owners are now aware that the fans expect at least one good fight on the field or they don't feel they got their money's worth."

Violence on the field has ebbed and flowed over the decades, but it has never been suppressed to the level anticipated by the Knickerbockers when they designed the game in the 1840s. The original Knickerbocker rules fined members for any cursing or vulgar displays. Cordiality and gentility have never been the norm, however. Baseball may be the most civil of American sports pastimes, but it is not a parlor game.

Connie Mack said that baseball in the 1880s, when he began his career playing catcher for Washington, "was thought, by solid sensible people, to be only one degree above grand larceny, arson, and mayhem." The even nastier 1890s were followed by a brief quiescent period when umpires, backed by baseball strongman Ban Johnson, returned some law and order to the game. W.A. Phelon in *Baseball Magazine* reacted in 1916:

> The games so far played, while of superior baseball quality, haven't been as fiercely and desperately contested, even when they went into extra innings, as those of earlier years.... Understand, this doesn't go as a plea for the return of rough stuff and vulgarity.... But I do say this, and challenge a denial: That the excessively strong legislation by which powers of high, low and middle justice are conferred upon the umpires, and the despotic style with which many of them now enforce their edicts, have tended to drive the life and spirit from the daily battles.... Base-

ball is a game of strong young men, and the red-blooded youth must kick when he thinks he gets the worst of anything.

The Attractiveness of Violence

It should not be surprising that we are entertained by violence, and baseball teaches us something about America's love for a good fight. Americans have always enjoyed a healthy scrap. Even when it was against the law, bare-knuckle prizefighting attracted huge crowds. Chess, by comparison, has a very small following; football, on the other hand, is a crushing success, a game that author John Fowles characterized as "the monotonous clashing armor of the brontosaurus." Jacques Barzun added: "To watch a football game is to be in prolonged neurotic doubt as to what you're seeing. It's more like an emergency happening at a distance than a game." Over the long run, baseball may just have the right amount of violence for American tastes.

Violence in sports mirrors violence in American society. It is not ever-present, but its potential exists. As a method for resolving disputes, maintaining control or demonstrating social power, physical violence has long prevailed across America in virtually all sectors of society. It was, and is, an everyday phenomenon, and, when not too dangerous, it can be very appealing and magnetic as a leitmotif for entertainment.

Baseball may be the least violent of the major team sports, but it has never been a peaceful repast. America's game released the violent side of the competitive spirit. At times, ballplayers seemed to be poisoned by their own testosterone, a testament to our bestial origins. Fans cheered loudest when opponents were not merely bested but beaten. Managers sought out players who would "mix it up." In 1892, for example, Cleveland Spiders manager Patsy Tebeau warned that "a milk-and-water, goody-goody player can't wear a Cleveland uniform." His club broke every rule, crossing from first to third base on a hit to the outfield, and tripping, punching, and holding opposing base runners. Even using every trick, Cleveland could only manage a third place finish in the twelve club circuit.

Leo Durocher, the controversial manager of the Dodgers and Giants, was a great believer in the value of purposeful mayhem on the field. A mediocre athlete during his years as a player, Durocher told the *Sporting News* in February 1961: "Some guys are admired for coming to play, as the saying goes. I prefer those who come to kill." Durocher's attitude towards the game was particularly aggressive and the lawless Dodgers of the early 1940s were Durocher's contribution to the history of violence in the major leagues. Branch Rickey said of Durocher, his Brooklyn manager: "He has the ability of taking a bad situation and making it immediately worse."

Survival in a harsh world — both inside and outside of baseball — made aggression a natural and necessary human trait. In reality, Americans have always lived in hostile places where violence was commonplace — whether urban, rural or alone on the frontier — and life has been perpetually unsafe for those who were careless. Violence, often preemptive, was necessary for existence. Modern life has eased the need for some of this belligerence, but certainly not all of it.

Many people bemoan the violence of modern American society, blaming television, movies and video games for the fact that America has the highest rate of homicides in the developed world. Most crimes here and elsewhere are perpetrated by young adult males. Youth violence in America may be a great national tragedy, but it is not a new phenomenon. Long before the media glorified combativeness, Americans learned to kill and maim each other at alarming rates. In 1852, the *New York Times* could look with sadness on the "unutterable squalor, vice and wretchedness" of the "den of thieves and murderers and prostitutes — the fountain of every imaginable abomination and every form of vice and crime" in sections of the nation's largest city.

Even the seemingly pastoral pastime of baseball has long experienced extremely violent episodes. In the pre-Knickerbocker days (when the game was sometimes called "rounders"), fielders would put a player out by throwing the ball at him when he was off his base. "Soaking" or "plugging" runners became a painful practice. As late as 1858, the rules of Massachusetts Town Ball (a different version of baseball that ultimately lost out to the Knickerbocker's New York form of the recreation) provided: "If a player, while running the Bases, be hit with the Ball thrown by one of the opposite side, before he has touched the home bound, while off a Base, he shall be considered out." One of the great innovations of the 1845 Knickerbocker rules was that they outlawed soaking. Forthwith, a runner had to be forced out or tagged out, or his batted ball caught on the fly or one bounce.

The Beanball

On Monday, August 16, 1920, the New York Yankees faced the Cleveland Indians at New York's Polo Grounds. Earlier that year, F.C. Lane, writing in *Baseball Magazine*, had reminded the fans of baseball that "Baseball...is a game indulged in by strong men, where give and take is not always defined within strict latitudes." That was evident that tragic day in Manhattan.

As the 1920 season approached its denouement, the Indians were charging for their first pennant, led by their engaging and well-liked shortstop Ray Chapman, and the Yankees were not far behind. The New Yorkers were also seeking their first pennant, and the competition was fierce. Chapman, who entered the game batting .303 with 97 runs scored, would normally crowd the plate. Carl Mays, the Yankees tough submarine-style starting pitcher, was unafraid to challenge hitters inside. Their encounter would change baseball history.

Both Mays and Chapman were born in rural Kentucky in 1891, but that was where their similarities ended. Chapman was a favorite of his teammates, and Mays was tolerated by his cohorts only because he was talented and competitive. At the top of the fifth inning, Chapman took his third turn at bat, crouching as usual close to the plate. It would be decades before batters wore helmets, first required by the National League in 1955 and by the American League one year later. Chapman stood no chance that late summer afternoon in 1920.

The Yankees starting pitcher Mays was well known as a surly and dangerous hurler. *Baseball Magazine* had written: "Mays has less 'stuff' than a whole raft of other boxmen, whom he outclasses in winning results, but his submarine delivery is mighty effective in torpedoing the batters." Mays delivered the submarine pitch from about dirt level on the mound, scrapping his knuckles on the ground. The pitch tailed up and into the batter. "Chappie" froze, defenseless, unable to move.

Yankees' third basemen Aaron Ward picked up the ball that seemed to have come off Chapman's bat and threw to first. In fact, the ball had struck Chapman directly in the temple. Chapman fell back towards the New York catcher and landed on his face bending over to his side. The umpire immediately called for a doctor, but as had happened thousands of times before, the batter bravely rose to cheers from the crowd and walked towards the visitor's clubhouse in deep centerfield. He collapsed around second base, unconscious. Blood ran out of his ears, nose and mouth. Mays's pitch had crushed his skull. Chapman's teammates carried him off the field. Emergency surgery removed a piece of his skull bone to relieve the pressure, but to no avail. Chapman died at 4:40 a.m. the next morning. The game scheduled for that day was cancelled.

The next day, the front page of the *Cleveland News* reported the loss of the "greatest shortstop, that is, considering all-around ability, batting, throwing, base running, bunting, fielding and ground covering ability, to mention nothing of his fight, spirit and conscientiousness, ever to wear a Cleveland uniform." Chapman had been a model citizen of the Forest City: "He was his 100 percent self all the time, no frills, or furbelows, and it was this trait that won him fast friends among the heads of manufacturing, industrial and mercantile concerns as well as among the newsies on the street corners." Chapman was also a splendid player. Statistical guru Bill James has concluded that Chapman was likely headed for the Hall of Fame had he completed his career.

The Indians persevered, despite the loss of their beloved sparkplug. Rookie Joe Sewell replaced Chapman at short, the start of his Hall of Fame career with the Indians. Cleveland players wore black armbands in tribute to their fallen teammate. Inspired by the loss of Chappie, the Indians won their first American League pennant and bested Brooklyn in the World Series. The club voted Ray Chapman's wife, Kathleen, a full

World Series share, just under $4,000. The tragic incident produced the only on-field fatality in the history of the major league game.

Carl Mays's pitches were hard for any batter to pick up on the way to the plate. Mays had also developed a well-earned reputation as a nasty competitor. Even Ty Cobb, who was not a favorite among many of his fellow ballplayers, disliked Mays and accused him of throwing pitches at batters: "I dodged a lot of them from him which made me darkly suspicious."

On September 16, 1915, at Fenway Park in Boston, Cobb and Mays squared off. Mays, relief pitching for the Sox before he was traded to the Yankees in 1919, curved two "rise-ball" pitches close to Cobb's head in the eighth inning. Cobb threw his bat at the pitcher, missing the mark, but making his point. Mays then hit him in the wrist, and Cobb took first. Cobb stole second, went to third on a ground out and home the same way, adding a sixth run to Detroit's total compared with Boston's single tally. The partisan crowd showed its hostility to Cobb by mobbing the outfielder as the game ended. Police escorted him off the field.

Cobb planned his retaliation against Mays carefully. Years later, Cobb dropped a bunt past Mays to the right of the pitcher's mound that would have to be fielded by the first baseman. Mays ran to cover the first base bag, only to be spiked by the charging Cobb. Cobb's spikes split open Mays' leg.

Like Cobb, Mays had a short fuse and was quick to anger. On Memorial Day in 1919 when the Red Sox played the Athletics in Philadelphia, Mays was sitting in the dugout when fans began to pound on its tin roof. Mays proceeded out of the dugout and flung a baseball into the crowd, hitting a fan in the head. The fan pressed criminal charges against Mays, who had left town and was not able to return until he publicly apologized.

Ray Chapman's tragic death left a positive legacy for baseball. Observers had seen a man mesmerized by the darkened on-coming pitch that sailed up to his head. Would Chapman have been able to see the ball heading to the plate if it had not been so scuffed by use over a period of innings? After the tragedy, league officials urged umpires to remove soiled balls from play. Batters benefited from having more visible (and perhaps more tightly-wound) horsehide to hit. The long ball explosion of the 1920s began, spurring new public interest in the game after Chapman's death and the subsequent revelation of the Black Sox scandal. From Chapman's death came the game's resurrection.

Although the only fatality at the major league level, Ray Chapman was not the only professional ballplayer to die playing the game. As early as 1862, pitcher James Creighton, a paid ringer with the Brooklyn Excelsiors, ruptured his bladder when he hit a home run in a game against the Morrisiana Unions. There was a loud pop sound just before his bat hit the ball. He rounded the bases before he collapsed. Carried off the field, Creighton died four days later from the internal hemorrhaging six months shy of his 22nd birthday. The stone marker above his grave in Brooklyn's Greenwood Cemetery was adorned with two crossed bats, a base, a cap and a scorecard. Baseball's first superstar died a martyr's death.

The *Reach Guide* of 1910 reported the following tragedy:

> At Dayton...September 14, 1909, during a double-header between the Dayton and Grand Rapids (Central League) teams, before the eyes of his aged father, who had traveled from Cleveland to watch his son's prowess on the ball field, and to take him home the next day to a family re-union, Charles Pinkney, second baseman and most popular member of the Dayton Club, was laid low by a terrific inshoot thrown by pitcher Hagerman in the last inning of the second game with Grand Rapids. Pinkney was taken to the hospital, where he died at noon the next day, without having recovered consciousness from a fractured skull. . . .

At least three other minor leaguers were struck and killed by thrown pitches in the years immediately preceding Chapman's death. One pitcher, Joseph Yeager of Fall River, Massachusetts, was even arrested in 1906 for manslaughter for beaning Tom Burke of Lynn, but the judge dismissed the charge. Even after the advent of the batting helmet, beanballs caused the death of three minor leaguers from 1956 to 1964.

Certainly, the death of Ray Chapman did nothing to deter pitchers from hurling inside to brush back batters. Even Carl Mays seemed unphased by what he had done. He continued his career, throwing inside for nine more seasons. In 1921, he led the American League pitchers with a 27-win campaign. Many think that Mays was ultimately not elected to the Hall of Fame because of Chapman's death, but others suggest that his reputation was sullied by allegations of game fixing in the 1921 World Series. It was later alleged that Mays' wife, sitting in the stands, signaled to her husband on the mound when she had received the promised bribe money by wiping her face with a handkerchief. An investigation could not pin the crime on the sidewinder.

Pre- and Postmortem

Despite the Chapman fatality, the beanball flourished in the national game. Deliberate beanballs and the injuries certain to follow have been part of the sport from the day pitchers were first allowed to throw overhand in 1883. In the earlier days of the game, pitchers began play by feeding balls to the batter underhanded. Before the Civil War, pitchers were expected to lob the pitch stiff-armed over home plate, and the pitch was to arrive where the batter could strike at it. A failed effort was considered unfair and subject to scorn by opponents and teammates alike.

At its inception, the game did not have a ball-and-strike count, but that was developed in the late 1850s and early 1860s to make sure the batter would have at least three (and in 1887, four) good pitches to strike at. The underhand rule evolved by the 1880s into a regulation that a pitch could not be delivered from above the pitcher's waist, although sidearm offerings were acceptable. To comply with this new standard and put some mustard on the ball, some pitchers even hiked their belts up close to their armpits!

In the 1870s pitchers began to throw harder. Joe Borden of the Philadelphia "Fillies" threw baseball's first no-hitter on July 19, 1875. Borden, who came from a prominent New Jersey family, often used the pseudonym Josephs because his parents disapproved of his playing ball.

He played for the Boston Red Caps during the first year of the National League, threw out his arm and ended the 1876 season as Boston's groundskeeper. By 1883, pitchers could throw sidearm from shoulder height. Within the decade, overhand pitching became the norm and with it, the potential to throw beanballs. With the advent of various "twirling" deliveries that caused the ball to jump and swerve, the American Association in 1884 finally instituted a rule that awarded first base to a batter hit by a pitch and the National League followed suit in 1887.

Pitchers understood the importance of keeping a batter unsettled. Jouett Meekin, a pitcher for the New York Giants in the 1890s, explained that to disturb a batter's confidence he would throw the first two pitches "within an inch of his head or body." When the batter stepped back out of harm's way, Meekin would throw him a curve on the outside of the plate. Remarkably, in his entire ten-year career of pitching more than 2600 innings, Meekin hit only 31 batters. During his brilliant 1894 season, Meekin and his fellow Giant pitcher Amos Rusie combined to pitch more than 90 complete games out of the 132 total games played by the club.

Rube Marquard, whose 18-year Hall of Fame career spanned the 1910s and 1920s, used the beanball to initiate rookies into the majors: "In those days you handled the young fellows all the same way. You threw a pitch at their heads to see if they could take it." Those who survived this dangerous rite of passage from the great pitcher presumably would be entitled to bat again and try to avoid another inside pitch.

In 1929, the Chicago Cubs won the pennant using three hurlers noted for their territorial imperative — to control the inside of the plate: Guy Bush, Pat Malone, and Charlie Root. Malone's high fastball was particularly dangerous. (Malone also fought 41 professional fights in the off-season under the name of Kid Williams.) The chant from the Cubs' players and fans rang out words of encouragement to the Chicago trio of hurlers: "Flatten 'em!" However, even this bevy of aggressive pitchers could not bring a World Series to the North Side of Chicago.

Brooklyn's spitballer, Burleigh Grimes, the aptly named husky Hall of Fame right-hander, had a stubby beard, a mean streak and an ornery reputation as a dirty player who hunted batters. Grimes held a grudge for a decade against Frankie Frisch, the Giants stalwart second baseman, because Frisch had the impertinence as a rookie to bunt successfully against Grimes for base hits. Frisch even had the temerity to spike Grimes once when he covered first base. Grimes tried without success to repay Frisch. "For the next ten years I aimed at least two balls at Frankie every time I pitched to him," Grimes later admitted. Finally, in a game in 1929 on a three-ball count when a pitcher would normally seek the strike zone, Grimes crunched a fast ball into Frisch's arm. The next year, Grimes and Frisch would both play for the St. Louis Cardinals and become "bosom pals," according to Grimes' later recollection.

Hugh Casey of the Brooklyn Dodgers in the 1940s was known to throw a pitch inside to a batter on occasion to force him off the plate. One day in the 1946 season, when he pitched in 46 games for the Dodgers, Casey even brushed back a player in the on-deck circle. Due to lead-off the inning for the Cardinals, shortstop Marty Marion stood six feet from the batter's circle timing Casey's deliveries with practice swings. Casey yelled at Marion to stop, but he would not. The next pitch sailed at Marion's head, sending him sprawling to the ground.

Great batters were not deterred by the risk of being hit by the pitch. Kid Eberfeld, an irascible infielder in the first decade of the twentieth century who was always ready to pick a fight, was hit on the head three times in one game. Starting in 1898, the "Peerless Leader," Frank Chance, played seventeen years in the majors. He too was notorious for crowding the plate at bat and freezing as a pitch sailed towards his head. Chance was hit 137 times in his career, and the repeated beanings finally took their toll. By the end of his playing days, Chance had lost his balance; he had developed a whine in his speech and suffered from headaches and double vision.

Many actual and potential Hall of Famers suffered similar fates, and it often cost them the twilight years of their careers. The Yankees' Bump Hadley thumped the Tigers' splendid catcher Mickey Cochrane above his right eye in 1937, breaking his skull in three places. Cochrane had homered off Hadley earlier in the game, and this was purposeful retaliation. Cochrane was knocked unconscious, and he never played baseball again. Always magnanimous, Cochrane exonerated Hadley: "I lost the ball. Hadley wasn't to blame."

The Cardinals Bob Bowman hit his former teammate Ducky Medwick in 1940 and nearly killed him. Medwick never regained the form that had made him the National League's Triple Crown winner in 1937, the last player in the senior circuit to lead the league in batting average, hits and runs-batted-in in the same season. Angels pitcher Jack Hamilton virtually ended young Red Sox hero Tony Conigliaro's career with a pitch that crushed his cheekbone in 1967. Conigliaro, the youngest home run champion in major league history, continued to play baseball, but not at his same level of excellence. When pitching for the Indians in 1995, Dennis Martinez hit the Twins stolid outfielder Kirby Puckett in the face. Puckett's jaw was broken, and he developed glaucoma in his right eye. He never played a regular major league game again.

Cochrane, Medwick and Puckett are enshrined in the Hall of Fame, and many observers think that Conigliaro, a truly gifted young athlete who posted Mantle-like statistics early in his career, had the potential to join them. They were all victims of the violence inherent in a sport where a hurler propels a ball hard as a rock at over 90 miles-per-hour towards a virtually defenseless batter.

"Fear," wrote Leonard Koppett in *A Thinking Man's Guide to Baseball*, "is the fundamental factor in hitting."

> The fear is simple and instinctive. If a baseball, thrown hard, hits any part of your body, it hurts. If it hits certain vulnerable areas, like elbows, wrist or face, it can cause broken bones and other serious injuries. If it hits a particular area of an unprotected head, it can kill. A thrown baseball, in short, is a missile, and an approaching missile generates a reflexive action: get out of the way. This fact . . . is the starting point for the game of baseball, and yet it is that least often mentioned by those who write about baseball.

The great pitchers know how to use that fear with skill. Sandy Koufax, one of the greatest ever, said: "Pitching is the art of instilling fear.

Show me a guy who can't pitch inside, and I'll show you a loser." Koppett wrote about Koufax's colleague, Don Drysdale: "He wanted the batter thinking: 'Hey, he's willing to kill me.'"

The Official Rules of Major League Baseball, of course, prohibit the beanball. Rule 8.02(d) proscribes an "intentional pitch at the batter." The Rules further provide by way of commentary:

> If, in the umpire's judgment, such a violation occurs, the umpire may elect either to:
>
> 1. Expel the pitcher, or the manager and the pitcher, from the game, or
>
> 2. May warn the pitcher and the manager of both teams that another such pitch will result in the immediate expulsion of that pitcher (or a replacement) and the manager. If, in the umpire's judgment, circumstances warrant, both teams may be officially "warned" prior to the game or at any time during the game.

Use of the pitch as a weapon, however, has not abated. As John P. Carmichael wrote in the *Chicago Daily News* in 1958: "It is virtually impossible to legislate against death, taxes and the beanball."

Ty Cobb

Baseball fanatics have always lauded the exploits of those players they considered fierce competitors. Foremost on that list is Tyrus Raymond Cobb, who ruled the base paths of the national game for more than two decades in the early twentieth century. Baseball, according to Cobb, was a "red-blooded sport," and he never shied away from the blood-letting. Cobb's targets were players and fans alike. Ty Cobb was a cruel and disturbed human being.

Cobb was also the game's most productive hitter throughout his career from 1907 until he retired in 1928. Power was not his game, as he choked up on his bat with his hands kept apart and slapped the pitcher's offerings through the holes in the infield. Once on base — something that happened quite often — Cobb was sure to run and certain to "dress out" with his spikes anyone who would stand in his way. "The base paths belonged to me," he exclaimed: "The rules gave me the right. I always went into a bag full of speed, feet first. I had sharp spikes on my shoes. If the baseman stood where he had no business to be and got hurt, that was his own fault." Many fielders left the game bloodied for having the temerity to challenge Cobb. As he later wrote, "In staking my claim, people were bound to get hurt."

On the 50th anniversary of Cobb's induction into the Hall of Fame, Jimmy Cannon wrote:

> The cruelty of Cobb's style fascinated the multitudes, but it also alienated them. He played in a climate of hostility, friendless by choice in a violent world he populated with enemies. Other players resented his calculated meanness. Their respect was reluctant but they were forced to present him with the trophy of their crabbed admiration. He was the strangest of all our national sports idols.

Cobb hated blacks, Catholics and Northerners, and he did not particularly like anyone else. He had to stay out of Ohio for more than a year after knifing a black waiter in Cleveland. In 1908, he paid $75 in damages for punching a black construction worker, considering it money well spent. He engaged in a fight almost every day with his teammates and with the public. When Tigers pitcher Ed Siever cursed at Cobb for not chasing after a fly ball, Cobb knocked his teammate down with a series of punches to the head, then kicked him in the face. Cobb slept each night with his gun. His advice to youngsters was plain and simple:

> The first requirement for a young fellow who hopes to make good in baseball is to have a good chin. Then he must stick that chin out about two extra inches and keep it there every minute of the time he is on the ball field. In other words, he must make up his mind to fight and then keep fighting.

He played the game, as he said, as if it was "not unlike a war."

The prospect of his violent revenge, Cobb believed, deterred opponents from confronting him in the first place:

I *did* retaliate. That I freely admit. If any player took unfair advantage of me, my one thought was to strike back as quickly and effectively as I could and put the fear of God into him. Let the other fellow fire the first shot, and he needed to be on the *qui vive* from then on. For I went looking for him. And when I found him, he usually regretted his act — and rarely repeated it. I commend this procedure to all young players who are of the aggressive type. The results are most satisfactory.

Even exhibition games counted in Cobb's book, at least in those years when he actually attended spring training. In a game against the New York Giants in 1916, Cobb spiked infielder Buck Herzog to retaliate for being brushed back from the plate. On first base, Cobb screamed at the Giants second baseman: "Now I'm coming down, you whore's son." Cobb's spikes ripped Herzog's uniform from the thigh to the ankle. At bat later in the game, Cobb responded to another inside pitch by challenging John McGraw's entire Giants team to a fight. Cobb and Herzog fought on the field, under the stands, and even in Cobb's hotel later that night. "I had to fight all my life to survive," Cobb later said, "They were all against me ... but I beat the bastards and left them in the ditch."

Cobb brought out the worst in his opponents. In a game in Cleveland in his second year in the majors, Cobb hit a ball to the outfield wall, circled the bases and headed home towards catcher Harry Bemis, who was waiting with the ball for his arrival. Cobb lowered his shoulder and pulverized Bemis, knocking the ball loose. Bemis retrieved the ball and attacked Cobb with it, until the umpire pulled Bemis off the runner and threw him out of the game. Cobb was not penalized. In a later contest, Cobb intentionally spiked Bemis in retaliation. As sportswriter Bozeman Bulger wrote: "He was possessed by the Furies." Or as Babe Ruth said more colorfully: "Ty Cobb is a prick."

One player who would stand up to Cobb was Honus Wagner, perhaps the greatest baseball player of all time. During the 1909 World Series, Cobb on first base yelled down to Wagner at shortstop: "I'm coming down on the first pitch, Krauthead." Wagner responded: "I'll be ready for you, Rebel." As usual Cobb slid into second base with his spikes high. Wagner took the throw from catcher George Gibson and tagged Cobb in the face, loosening three teeth: "We also play a little rough in our league, Mr. Cobb."

Rowdyism on the Field

The original Orioles of Baltimore were feared and famed for their rowdy playing strategy. *New York Times* sportswriter Joe Durso described Orioles baseball in the 1890s as "a combination of hostility, imagination, speed and piracy." John Heydler, an umpire in the 1890s who later became the president of the National League, remembered the Orioles as "mean, vicious, ready to maim a rival player or an umpire, if it helped their cause." Foremost among the offenders was John McGraw, who would spike an umpire through his shoe in order to make his point.

McGraw had a quick temper and a strong punch. The many opponents he fought included Willie Keeler, Ad Brennan, Ty Cobb, and Bill Byron, "The Singing Umpire," who would sing some of his calls behind the plate. In 1894, in his third year in the game, McGraw kicked Boston Beaneater first baseman Tommy Tucker in the head after applying the tag at third base. Tucker, egged on by the local crowd, lashed out at McGraw. The crowd focused on the melee, ignoring the fact that a fire had broken out at Boston's South End Grounds. The fire, started when a fan dropped a cigarette through the seats in right field, burned the grandstand to the ground and leveled hundreds of neighborhood homes.

Ned Hanlon, the Orioles club owner and manager, explained to the *New York Clipper* on May 25, 1895:

> Ball players are not school children, nor are umpires school masters. It is impossible to prevent expressions of impatience or actions indicating dissent with the umpire's decision when a player, in the heat of the game, thinks he has been unjustly treated....

Patrons like to see a little scrappiness in the game, and would be dissatisfied, I believe, to see the players slinking away like whipped school-boys to their benches, afraid to turn their heads for fear of a heavy fine from some swelled umpire.

Not every star of the game would find it necessary to "kick" at the umpires in order to prove his manhood and dominance. Honus Wagner, for one, avoided those disputes and simply played the game to perfection. The Dutchman opined: "In all my years of play, I never saw an ump deliberately make an unfair decision. They really called them as them saw 'em." The 1884 *Spalding Guide*, edited by Father Chadwick during those years, preached "against the player or captain who indulges his bad temper by kicking" against an umpire's call.

Whenever you see a player or a captain who has made misplays and wants to throw the onus of it on the umpire, you will find your stupid, short-sighted kicker at work, sure. Some of these days, when the game gets out of the ruts of one kind or another it now wallows in, we will see the folly of kicking done away with. Captains of professional teams have been disputing decisions, which cannot possibly be reversed, for so long a time that it has become a sort of second nature to them.

The *Guide* would repeat this entreaty almost annually until it ceased publication in 1939.

Protesting an umpire's call remains a unique part of the baseball experience, although rarely does a protester actually touch the umpire. In what other sport does a manager or coach run out to the field of play while time is called to hurl epithets (or even throw dirt) at the appointed neutral who obviously had suddenly turned blind? Fans expect their team's leader to partake of this normally fruitless task and, if the spirit moves him, to be sufficiently outrageous to be tossed from the contest. The scene is repeated daily, and fans never seem to tire of the show. It has an ancient origin. In the *Beadle Dime Baseball Player* in 1860, Father Chadwick wrote: "The position of an umpire is an honorable one, but its duties are anything but agreeable, as it is next to an impossibility to give entire satisfaction to all parties concerned in a match." The *New York Evening World* in 1923 reported that umpires have had a "czaristic temper" since 1845.

John McGraw's counterpart and the greatest "kicker" of modern times was the irrepressible Billy Martin, the great Yankee second baseman and long-time major league manager. Martin preached hustle to his charges, even if that meant going over the edge. Martin told the *Sporting News* in 1968: "The day I become a good loser, I'm quitting baseball. . . . I always had a temper. I think it's nothing to be ashamed of. If you know how to use it, it can help."

For their part, umpires have never shied away from confrontation. Umpire Tim Keefe even had eight members of the Cleveland Spiders arrested during a game in June 1896. In the early days, the *New York Evening World* reported, umpires did not have to make instant decisions: "the umpire had time to stroke his whiskers, lift his top hat, scratch his head in thought, and then, placing his hand picturesquely on his hip, with one foot poised on a chair, say in dulcet tones — so that the girls in crinolines on the lawns of the Elysian Field might hear — "Out."

As the game developed, however, instant — and correct — decisions were expected. In direct response to these ever-present challenges, umpires claimed infallibility. As umpire Ed Runge once explained to *Sports Illustrated*: "It's the only occupation where a man has to be perfect the first day on the job and then improve over the years." *Time Magazine* wrote in 1961 that the perfect umpire "should combine the integrity of a Supreme Court justice, the physical ability of an acrobat, the endurance of Job and the imperturbability of Buddha."

Very few umpires come close to that ideal. One who was willing to acknowledge his shortcomings was Ron Luciano, who admitted to the *Chicago Tribune* in 1982:

A lot of calls are guesses. They have to be. . . . With balls and strikes, it's impossible to get them right all the time. I mean every major-league pitch moves some way or another. None go straight, not even the fastballs.

Ballplayers found umpires arrogant and offensive, and they were. Although some umpires, like Jocko Conlan, could demand respect on the field, managers and players felt compelled to challenge their authority. Baiting the umpire has been part of the game of baseball since the 1880s. To complain about the performance of the umpires seemed only natural. The phrase "kill the ump" was a common crank call dating from that era. Few players, however, reached the depths of the Phillies left fielder Sherry Magee on July 10, 1911. Magee argued vociferously when umpire Bill Finneran called him out on strikes. He then swung and broke the umpire's jaw. Magee was fined and suspended for five weeks. At the end of his playing days, Magee returned to the major leagues as an umpire himself.

Baltimore second baseman Roberto Alomar came close to the level of Magee's perfidy. After being called out on a third strike in September 1996, Alomar first argued with umpire John Hirschbeck and exchanged unpleasantries — a typical rhubarb. Alomar then spit on Hirschbeck. Three days later, Alomar issued a formal apology: "I deeply regret my disrespectful conduct toward a man that I know always gives his utmost as an umpire.... I'm sincerely sorry that my actions deeply offended John and, by engaging in indefensible conduct, I failed the game of baseball, the Orioles organization and my fellow major leaguers." Suspended for five days by League President Gene Budig, Alomar donated his earnings in that period to charity.

Although perhaps the most famous spit, Alomar's expectoration was not the first in baseball history directed at a neutral in black. In 1939 at a game at the Polo Grounds, Giants shortstop Billy Jurges spit on umpire George Magerkurth's face. The umpire retaliated with a punch to the jaw. National League president Ford Frick fined both Jurgis and Magerkurth $250 and suspended them for ten days. Actually, the saliva has flowed both ways in baseball history. On August 4, 1909, umpire Tim Hurst spat on Eddie Collins when the Hall of Famer disputed one of Hurst's calls. A riot ensued. Hurst's only comment: "I don't like college boys." (Collins had attended Columbia University.) Two weeks later, Hurst was banished from baseball.

Baseball Violence and the American Identity

When the on-field violence of the National Game is laid before us, we can certainly question whether it represents the best of the American condition. Mayhem on the base paths, intentional assaults with bats and balls, fights and fury without much provocation — this is part of the picture of baseball that appears over time. Not every pitcher is hunting for heads, of course, but some are, and most hurlers brush back batters if they are to become successful on the mound. Not all players get into fights, but players generally do not turn the other cheek.

We know that it takes personal physical and emotional strength to be successful, and those qualities are certainly essential on the ball field. No one ever handed out success, and opportunity lies open only for those with courage and skill. As Branch Rickey noted perceptively: "Luck is the residue of design." Design requires both ability and a willingness to stand up and take risks. That raises your chances whether in life or on the field of play.

Ty Cobb jumped into the stands at New York's Hilltop Park to attack a physically-disabled heckler sitting twelve rows up, pummeling him with punches and kicks from his spikes, leaving him a bruised and bloody mess.

Chapter 6

Violence Beyond the Playing Field

What is both surprising and delightful is that spectators are allowed, and even expected, to join in the vocal part of the game.... There is no reason why the field should not try to put the batsman off his stroke at the critical moment by neatly timed disparagements of his wife's fidelity and his mother's respectability. – George Bernard Shaw

EDWARD MOSS, writing for *Harper's Weekly* in 1910, waxed eloquently about the unique nature of the American baseball fan:

> Awakening from his hibernation at the first call of "Play Ball!" the baseball fan stretches and takes his place with his fellows among the long tiers of pine planks. His winter of discontent is past.... Indigenous to America, no other country can produce his like. Tsar and serf combined, he makes professional baseball possible and is slave to the sport he dominates.... Business and professional men forget for the time their standing in the community and, shoulder to shoulder with the street urchin, "root" frantically for the hit needed to win the game.... It is seldom that there is any demonstration that extends beyond vocal outbreaks and these are quickly nipped in their conception by the special officers who are on duty in every ballpark of the big circuits.

Apparently, Moss's idealized fans were not in attendance two years later at the Polo Grounds in New York. By the fourth inning of Detroit's game against the New York Highlanders on May 15, 1912, Ty Cobb had exhausted his slim portion of patience. Cobb jumped into the stands at New York's Hilltop Park to attack a heckler sitting twelve rows up. Cobb did not know, nor did he care, that his target, Claude Lueker, was physically disabled. It was sufficient for him that his victim had called Cobb names. Cobb later explained his personal philosophy: "There are some epithets that no decent man will stand for under any circumstances. When any man applied them to me, he must be prepared to lick me or take a licking."

Lueker was a former newspaper pressman who had lost eight fingers in a workplace accident and could not defend himself. Cobb "johnny-kilbaned" the spectator, according to the *New York Times*, pummeling him with punches and kicks from his spikes, and leaving him a bruised and bloody mess. The press put the blame squarely on the shoulders of the heckler who used language "that has no place in a family newspaper or even one that circulates in barber shops only." The paper reported that when Cobb was told his adversary had no hands, Cobb replied: "I don't care if he has no feet." The umpire had to enter the stands to pull Cobb off his victim and put Cobb out of the game.

American League President Ban Johnson was at the park that day and witnessed Cobb's attack on the spectator. He suspended the outfielder indefinitely. Cobb complained to the *Atlanta Constitution* that a "great injustice" had been done and he should have had an opportunity to be heard before the sentence was imposed: "I tried to avoid this man, but when his language became too much for me to stand, I lost my head." He later told the *Constitution*: "[T]hat fellow sure had me mad. . . . I'll bet he will never repeat that dose of profanity in a ballpark."

Although newspapers across the country reported the suspension, few explained what had set off the Georgia Peach. Lueker had called out to all the Tiger players, saying they ought to be ashamed playing with a "half nigger." He said that Cobb was a "half coon." Cobb could not stand the racial taunts. He told the *Atlanta Constitution*: "He had worked me into such a frenzy that I guess I beat him up pretty bad." The crowd cheered as Cobb left the field. His manager, Hugh Jennings, explained: "I heard the remark, but I knew it would be useless to restrain Ty, as he would have gotten his tormenter sooner or later. When Ty's Southern blood is aroused he is a bad man to handle." The next day, Cobb explained: "A ball player, however, should not be expected to take everything, as we have some self-respect and we cannot endure more than human nature will stand for." He had no regrets.

A few days later, Lueker explained what had occurred, ignoring his provocative heckling:

> He let out with his fist and caught me on the forehead, over the left eye. You can see the big bump over there now. I was knocked over, and then he jumped me. He spiked me in the left leg and kicked me in the side. Then he booted me behind the left ear. I saw that the Detroit players were wading into the crowd with their bats, but I did not see anybody hit. I was down and couldn't see much anyway. Then the fuss was broken up.

Cobb's teammates, none of whom considered the irascible star a friend, but all of whom recognized the importance of his bat in the lineup, declared that they would not play unless Cobb was reinstated. They telegraphed President Johnson:

> Feeling Mr. Cobb is being done injustice by your action in suspending him, we the undersigned refuse to play another game after today until such action is adjusted to our satisfaction. He was fully justified in his action, as no one could stand such personal abuse from anyone.

Even Manager Hugh Jennings told the press that the suspension was not warranted: "The players should be protected from objectionable spectators." The Tigers next opponent, the members of the world-champion Athletics, threatened to join in the "mutiny." The players should "stand together," they told the *Chicago Daily Tribune*, "and insist that some protection should be afforded them against insults hurled at them by irresponsible rooters."

Ban Johnson remained adamant. Rowdyism at the ball field would not be countenanced. He refused to budge on the suspension and ordered the Tigers to take the field to play their scheduled contest. Backed by the American League owners who recognized that the spontaneous work stoppage by the Tigers could foster the formation of a players union, Johnson suspended all the strikers and called off one scheduled game. The Tiger players showed up in uniform for the next scheduled game on May 18 against the Athletics, but then refused to play. Detroit played one game with substitute players drawn from the local colleges and sandlots, but lost that sham contest 24–2.

Detroit club president "Lucky Frank" Navin promised his players that he would pay any fines imposed on them if they returned to play. After Cobb personally urged them to return, the strike collapsed. The League fined each participant $100, a sum that Navin paid as he had promised. Finally, after further investigation, President Johnson concluded that the "direct responsibility for the unfortunate occurrence rests upon the player," and fixed Cobb's suspension at ten days with a fine of $50. Cobb, according to Johnson, had been the first "to employ vicious language" in the incident and did not first seek redress "by appeal to the umpire." Instead, Cobb took the law into his own hands. Johnson warned all players not to act as "judge and avenger of real or fancied wrongs while on duty." Even with Cobb back in the lineup, the Tigers ended the 1912 season in sixth place, although Cobb won another batting title with a .409 average.

The public and the press supported Cobb, their baseball hero, in this struggle. *Baseball Magazine* concluded "It was the fan who caused the trouble." Lueker's scurrilous language was "an unjustifiable attack on an unoffending player." On the other hand, although "Cobb did what was natural," his action "was doubtlessly mistaken." The law of baseball should be enforced. The Tiger players' strike was "sadly impracticable." The publication applauded the actions of all concerned (except Lueker), praising Cobb and magnate Navin in particular. This was not a mere fleeting incident, however. "It was a case of Individual Liberty versus Organized Authority," and organized authority won with hardly a struggle.

The Proper Place

To flourish as the American pastime, baseball needs both players and fans. They each have their appropriate roles and places — the former to offer the athletic exhibition on the field, the latter to watch it from the stands. Over the 160 year history of American baseball, however, unruly and normally beer-besotted fans have intruded upon the sanctity of the baseball diamond and players, like Cobb, have entered the fans' domain. That can be a risky adventure both for the fans and for the players.

Normally, attention-seeking buffoons who run out on the playing field are quickly dispatched by security and briskly ejected from the park. That did not happen, however, on Opening Day, April 11, 1907, at the Polo Grounds. More than a thousand fans rushed the field after the bottom of the eighth inning. They amused themselves by throwing bottles, glasses and cushions. The *New York Times* suggested that the crowd likely was reacting to the umpire's previous efforts to clear some fans from the field. Fortunately, the invading horde was good-natured and enjoyed its prank. Hundreds more soon joined the men and boys who had jumped the ropes and frolicked on the field. When the under-manned police contingent could not clear the field in 15 minutes, the umpires ruled that the Giants had forfeited the game to the Phillies. (The Giants were losing 3–0 in any case and had accumulated but one hit.) No one was arrested.

Almost a century later, in April 2005, the Boston Red Sox imposed a serious punishment on a fan who interfered with play. Yankee right fielder Gary Sheffield attempted to play the carom off the low right field wall at Fenway Park, and the fan in Row A, Box 86, Section 4, near the right-field foul pole reached over and, according to the player, hit him in the mouth. Security reacted immediately, sprinting from the nearby bullpen. Fortunately, Sheffield restrained himself or it could have become a very nasty incident. The fan with the great seats, later identified as Christopher House, was quickly escorted from the park. Sheffield, known for his temper, later applauded his own achievement: "I'm just glad I was an example of how to handle a situation." Yankees manager

Joe Torre offered: "These people shouldn't be allowed to walk the street, much less come to a ballgame." The following month, a Boston clerk magistrate ruled that there was insufficient evidence to charge the fan with even a misdemeanor for disorderly conduct. The Sox, however, pulled the spectator's season tickets, a private penalty for his felony comparable, at least for Sox fans, to life imprisonment without parole.

Sports fans at the ballpark are not expected to be angels sitting serenely at church while the anointed in their vestments perform the rituals of the game. Paul Gallico's 1944 book of essays, *Farewell to Sport*, brilliantly captured the unique role of baseball enthusiasts at the ballpark:

> [T]he crowd as a whole plays the role of Greek chorus to the actors on the field below. It reflects every action, every movement, every changing phase of the game. It keens. It rejoices. It moans. It jeers. It applauds and gives great swelling murmurs of surprise and appreciation. . . . It is the next best thing to participation.

For many fans, the games on the field take on a monumental importance and produce irrational results, even in the absence of libation. After the third game of the 1911 World Series, depressed by an eleventh inning loss by his beloved Giants to the Athletics, 14-year-old Allen McGyre ran away from home and was found hours later sprawled across the trolley tracks. That same year, the *New York Times* bemoaned in "The Wreck of the Fan," a mythical adherent found babbling at the shore, muttering about what could have been. Old-timers always commiserate that the game just isn't what it used to be. Sometimes the excitement is just too much. On August 20, 1930, Harry Pumpian, a Cubs fan, was on his feet cheering for most of the game against the Brooklyn Robins. He worked himself into a frenzy as the Cubs threatened to win the game in the bottom of the eleventh inning. The Cubs scored and Pumpian collapsed from the excitement. He was pronounced dead by the Cubs physician.

A History of Sports Disorder

Violence involving spectators at sporting events is not a new phenomenon. In Roman times, supporters of opposing teams in the chariot races often engaged in major riots. In Constantinople in 532 A.D., for example, followers of the Blues, Reds, Greens, and Whites engaged in complete mayhem. Emperor Justinian I, a supporter of the Blues, was forgiving at first. He commuted all the death sentences. The fans demanded a full pardon. They attacked their prison and set Constantinople ablaze, shouting the racing cheer *nika* ("victory"). Justinian put down the uprising with a death toll that approached 30,000.

Roman blood sports always relied on violence as the main attraction. Killing human beings and animals was the daily fare. Gladiatorial combat, the execution of foreigners, slaves, and wild beasts topped the bill. When Emperor Caligula ran out of gladiators, he simply ordered the spectators in a section of the grandstand into the ring to battle to the death! Modern soccer matches also pose physical dangers to spectators and players alike. At the FA Cup semifinal in 1989 in Sheffield, U.K., 95 fans were crushed to death. In Guatemala in 1996 in a World Cup qualifying match 80 people were killed in a stampede. In 1964 in the worst soccer disaster on record, more than 300 fans were killed and over 500 injured in a riot in Lima, Peru. For the most part, baseball has escaped the fate of both the coliseum sports and soccer bedlam.

That does not mean that baseball fans do not take their contests seriously. Anyone who has experienced the Red Sox-Yankees rivalry would attest to the fact that aspersions about a wife's fidelity or a mother's respectability would constitute the least of the spectators' verbal offenses. Home clubs heighten security to address the fights that sometimes break out in the stands between loyalists of the two teams, especially after many innings of beer consumption. Boston and New York have been rivals on the diamond since the earliest days of the organized game. Adherents of both clubs have always known the game well. As the *Boston Globe* reported on Opening Day 1887: "It was the same old crowd. It knew ball.... A little base ball now and then is relished by the wisest men." Wisdom may be lost, however, in the face of baseball partisanship.

We should not ignore the fact that even when fans and players behave and the game is played according to the rules, spectating can be dangerous. Owners have always warned attendees about the risks of foul balls. A ball hit on a line into the stands can be lethal, and it has been on at least five occasions. The front page of the *Los Angeles Times* on May 21, 1970, reported one of those deaths. A fourteen year old boy, Alan Fish, died as a result of a foul ball at Dodger Stadium. Fish and his friends had attended every home game of the season and he had always brought his mitt. The balls never came his way and eventually he would leave his glove at home. He leaned forward from his second row seat behind first base to take a bite out of his hot dog as Manny Moto took his turn at bat. A foul ball clipped the youngster above his left ear. He lapsed into a coma later that night and died the next afternoon. His parents sued the Dodgers for a million dollars for its failure to provide their son "with a safe place to witness the ballgame" at Dodger Stadium, but the Dodgers prevailed in the litigation.

Perhaps the most remarkable foul ball fatality occurred in the minor league ballpark in Morristown, Ohio. Stanton Walker was keeping score of the game when he asked his companion for a knife to sharpen his pencil. Walker took the knife and before he could sharpen his writing implement he was hit in the hand by a line drive. The ball drove the knife into Walker's heart. Walker fell to the ground dead, the knife sticking in his heart and his hand still clasping the handle.

Many fans are injured as a result of stray liners, but few enjoyed the bad luck of Alice Roth. A foul ball off the bat of Richie Ashburn, the great center fielder for the Phillies, hit Mrs. Roth, the wife of Earl Roth, the sports editor of the Philadelphia Bulletin. The ball broke her nose. When the club attendants carried Mrs. Roth out on a stretcher, Ashburn lined another pitch toward the area and hit her once again while she was lying on the stretcher.

The American Enterprise

In a comparatively short period of time in the nineteenth and early twentieth century, America absorbed millions of immigrants from other countries who fundamentally altered the nature of its established society. The original settlers — primarily from England, Scotland and Wales — were joined by other Europeans and Asians who came to find a better life or escape from a worse one. Each group brought its own mores, values, language and religion. As Whitman said, "Here is not merely a nation, but a teeming nation of nations."

Nineteenth century baseball cranks were a potpourri of classes and ethnic groups, most drawn from those immigrant clans. Although some members of the gentry attended the game and sat in the equivalent of luxury boxes at premium prices, fans of the National Game, for the most part, were the denizens of urban immigrant neighborhoods who worked long hours under difficult working conditions to earn the money to attend the contests. Baseball at the major league level was played in the large cities of the East and Midwest where the immigrants had settled. For a century, St. Louis, in the center of the continent, was the southern-most and western-most outpost of the sport at the major league level.

From its inception, America was a land where physical violence often ruled over reason and where public regulation took second place to private ordering. Life in nineteenth century urban America was particularly noxious and dangerous. Pollution and disease were constant and unstoppable. It was a boisterous torrent of sights and sounds. When Oscar Wilde visited the East Coast cities in 1882, he said: "America is the noisiest country that ever existed." Wilde also found the American habit of incessant spitting quite repulsive, as well as the public's penchant to "take their heroes from the criminal classes."

Private associations of men ran urban ethnic neighborhoods. These organized gangs served a variety of social purposes. Although their activities were often nefarious, they were not solely criminal enterprises. These organizations served social needs and captured the political process to achieve their purposes. In the presence of ineffective and corrupted police protection, the maintenance of public safety often depended on the most unsafe of institutions, the neighborhood gang.

Boss Tweed's all-powerful Tammany organization in mid-nineteenth century New York City was a perfect example. It began as a volunteer fire company, of all things. There were no publicly-funded fire brigades in fire-prone New York City at the time. The market for fire protection encouraged the creation of private associations — there were many in addition to Tweed's boys — that would offer their services for payment at the site of a blazing structure. When two or more fire companies arrived at the scene, they would engage in fist fights to determine which group had the right to contract for fire suppression. During these preliminaries, buildings might simply burn to the ground.

We should add one more critical element to the nineteenth-century urban scene — the saloon. Compared with the dreadful living conditions at home in the slums, saloons offered a well-lit space for male socializing after long hours at work. The beer and whiskey were not polluted, as the drinking water often was. One direct result of these ubiquitous nineteenth century social institutions was public drunkenness on a large scale. Freed of inhibitions, in close proximity to others similarly inebriated, the urban male posed a physical threat to fellow imbibers and to himself.

It should not be surprising to discover that when these urbanites visited the ballpark they posed a similar threat to other attendees. They did not suddenly reform when passing through the gates (or over the fence) to the field of play. Whiskey was first made available at baseball games in New York City in the 1870s. Although the National League prohibited selling alcoholic beverages at its inception in 1876, the American Association did not join in the ban during its ten-year run (1882–1891) as the principal rival professional baseball circuit. In any case, no one has suggested that the National League grandstands were dry, only that no liquor was sold legally on the premises.

Combine a predisposition for the use of physical force with the lubrication of alcohol and a passion for their local baseball nines, and the combination foretold tumble and turmoil. Inebriated and excited by the action on the field and accustomed to engaging in the physical fray, the cranks participated in the baseball game in their own way. George Bernard Shaw was correct about their verbal displays, but they also disturbed the game on the field, hurling various objects and even entering upon the diamond. Fans took it upon themselves to help their clubs win.

On the Field

In the early days of the professional game, spectators would regularly invade the field of play. In the days before enclosed stadiums, the onlookers stood outside the baselines and in the outfields. Fights among members of the crowd would pour on to the field disrupting play. Albert Spalding described these cranks as "utterly uncontrollable elements of thugs, gamblers, thieves, plug-uglies and rioters" who would often "show bad temper." On June 14, 1870, during the Cincinnati Red Stockings' second national tour, it was reported that a Brooklyn die-hard fanatic in right field jumped on Cincinnati outfielder Calvin McVey to keep him from making a rally-ending catch of a fly ball. Two runs scored for the Brooklyn Atlantic club and the batter ended up at third base. The *New York Times* rued "the miserable partisan character of the assemblage which was the most discreditable gathering we have seen on the Capitoline Grounds for many years." Only later would baseball create a rule penalizing the home team for fan interference.

Fights among spectators were a common occurrence during and after games. Operators thought that raising admission prices might eliminate patronage from members of the lower classes who were thought more prone to such misconduct. Either the hypothesis was wrong or the violence was a product of all classes. Baseball cranks came to watch, gamble and fight.

Henry Chadwick criticized his fellow sports journalists for their elaborate descriptions of the fights in the grandstands. This, Chadwick argued, only encouraged "those who in a crowd of spectators at a ball match, at the cry of 'fight, fight,' rush from the manly excitements of such a contest to seek gratification for their brutal tastes in witnessing and encouraging bloody encounters between two or three blackguards." Chadwick believed that baseball had the potential of developing good moral habits in both the participants and the spectators. He regretted the effect of greed on the sport, and instead promoted his panglossian vision of unsullied athletics. At times, however, even Father Chadwick had to acknowledge that the facts of the matter were far more disheveled.

Baseball attracted the roughs and rowdies who brought their penchant for fisticuffs to the fields where the games were played. Life in urban America could be riotous, and lower-class gangs roamed the streets and the ball fields. In 1865, Chadwick, writing for the *New York Clipper*, acknowledged that baseball could do well without these ruffians, these members of the "blackleg fraternity." Young thugs were attracted by the crowds, the rapid action of the sport and the opportunity to consume alcohol in public. By the 1890s, management in some ballparks enclosed the grandstand with tall barbed wire fences. Kept from the field, crowds would attack visiting ballplayers after the game and mob their carriages. It could be a frightening scene.

Danger at the Ballpark

It was sometimes dangerous simply to attend a baseball game. In addition to the deaths caused by foul balls, at least one fan died from an errant throw. On September 30, 1943, during a night game in the Nation's Capital, Washington Senators third baseman Sherry Robertson threw wildly over Mickey Vernon's outreached glove and hit 32-year-old Clarence D. Stagemyer, seated in the front row behind first base. The ball fractured his skull. He died four hours later.

Poorly built or maintained stadiums also exacted their toll. Water had rotted out a wooden walkway on the promenade at the Phillies Philadelphia baseball park. It collapsed on August 9, 1903, causing nine deaths. Two hundred fans were seriously injured. John Rogers, the owner of the Phillies, dismissed the event as "one of those accidents that occur when a large number of people actuated by a common impulse do something unexpected." Two lawsuits were filed immediately and soon settled.

New York City baseball parks have been particularly dangerous places to attend games. On May 19, 1929, fans in the Yankee Stadium bleachers in the Bronx stampeded for the exit when a deluge of rain caused a flood. Two fans, a Hunter College sophomore, Eleanor Price, and Joseph Carter, a 60-year-old truck driver, were killed in the crush and 62 others were injured. Some fans fell at the exit way and others piled on top of them. "The scene was one rivaled only by a medieval painting of horror," wrote the *Chicago Tribune*. Many of those injured were young boys who congregated, as usual, in "Ruthville" beyond the right field fence where the Babe lofted his homers. Their husky hero had obliged with a round tripper in the third inning, before the tragedy struck.

On July 4, 1950, a shot rang out at the Polo Grounds and Barney Doyle of Fairview, New Jersey, a former boxing manager, was struck and killed. The shooter could not be identified. There was some thought that the stray bullet had come from a neighborhood holiday celebration. A man who identified himself as a doctor examined the small hole above Doyle's left eyebrow and announced "that man's dead." He then disappeared back into the crowd to enjoy the Giants-Dodgers contest. Doyle's body was removed to Bellevue Hospital and his seat was immediately seized by a standee.

Fans often get into arguments during and after games, although they do not always prove fatal. On September 19, 2003, however, Giants and Dodgers fans argued in the Chavez Ravine parking lot after the Giants victory. Manuel Hernandez, the Dodgers fan, shot Mark Antenorcruz, the Giants adherent, in the chest and he died at the scene.

Violence in America

Much like today, the newspapers of the nineteenth century were filled with stories about crime. On January 4, 1865, the *New York Times* reported there had been an "unconscionable number of murderous assaults on New Year's Day...nearly all of them the fruits of immoderate indulgence in intoxicating liquors." Barney Frierley, a saloonkeeper on Houston Street, had murdered a patron, a prizefighter named Harry Lazarus, by cutting his throat with a razor. A week later, the *Times* worried: "Crime in New York — What Shall Be Done!" In the prior year, 500 homicides were attempted in the City, 100 of which were successful:

> In fact, human life seems to be every day held in less and less respect in our dangerous classes....[T]here is apparent among the rowdies an increasing disposition to use deadly weapons either in deciding their quarrels, or in aiding their robberies, or merely in satisfying their destructiveness.

"Skylarking" young men would create mayhem in the community, even if their intent was not murderous. Every day the press reported on the continued decline of the American civilization.

The American experience had always been thoroughly infused with violence. All were aware that life in this country was filled with uncertainty and unforeseeable contingencies. America was settled by waves of mostly Old World immigrants, and soon became an amalgam of subcultures, at times living in harmony with one another, but often in conflict for economic, social and religious advantage. At the turn of the twentieth century, the average life span in America was only 43 years for whites and 33 years for blacks, about half of what it is today. About half of all children lost a parent before the age of 16. Half of all parents lost at least one child. Although disease was the primary cause of most premature deaths, violence was the ever present alternative. Many unpleasant things happened.

The United States was founded as a slave country, relying on the forced bondage of human beings for its very economic existence. Slavery needed state-sanctioned violence in order to exist. The American agrarian economy prospered because the unpaid source of labor brought profits to all, including Northern commercial interests who participated fully in the fruits of the slave system. The much-celebrated

174

frontier experience where individual accomplishment and bravery paid handsome dividends was the exception, when it was true at all. The prevailing myth of the frontier ignored the reality — the systematic exclusion and ultimately the extermination of native peoples who had settled the continent centuries before the Europeans.

Urban America, a mostly Northern phenomenon, became a hotbed of gang and mob violence. The Plug Uglies, the Hartley Mob, and the Molasses Gang ruled sections of New York City in the nineteenth century. Their counterparts controlled portions of all other cities. For the most part, members of the gangs of the eastern cities were Irish, but other ethnic clans organized their own defensive groups. Men joined together in the face of poverty, squalid conditions, and abiding prejudice. The product of unhealthy slums and malnutrition, the gangs exercised enormous political influence because of their ability and willingness to use violence to maintain dominance and produce votes at election time.

Migration from farms and immigration from foreign countries brought millions to America's urban slums to work in the factories. Some were fortunate to procure white collar positions as service clerks, but most joined the workforce without the prospect of any steady employment. Much urban disorder in the nineteenth century was the product of rowdies and so-called "corner hangers." Simple disorderly conduct, often the product of excessive consumption of alcohol rather than open warfare, was the norm. Some of these toughs joined volunteer fire departments, but were more interested in the fisticuffs than the fire suppression. Some rowdy behavior led to murder and assault charges. Most criminal acts simply went unpunished.

American cities grew without the essential infrastructure of water and sewers. Disease was rampant. Packs of domesticated animals and rodents scavenged freely in the streets. A New York City newspaper painted the scene: "The offal and filth, of which there are loads thrown from the houses in defiance of an ordinance which is never enforced, is scraped up with the usual deposits of mud and manure into big heaps and left for weeks together on the sides of the streets." Nineteenth century urbanites understood that the stench or miasmas produced by the manure piles posed a serious health hazard, but cleaning was sporadic at best.

Violence was not the only agent of death in a changing America. Few families went unscathed by pestilence and disease borne of the absence of sanitation. Urban living conditions were wretched. The absence of medical care meant that contagion was a certain death sentence. Fire was also a genuine threat. Urban lives and possessions were often lost as the conflagration moved through a city. The one constant was that life was contingent, based on unseen forces that at any moment could destroy the life of a family or many families. America had become, according to the *Washington Post*, the "dumping ground" of humanity.

America was always a profoundly religious country, ruled by sectarianism much like the rest of the Western world. Religion caused differences, discrimination and despair. America's religious freedom was more fabled than real. America was a Protestant Christian commonwealth and this hegemony was sometimes maintained by violence. Lyman Beecher and Horace Bushnell incited their Protestant followers to attack immigrant Catholics when they first arrived in numbers in the 1830s and 1840s. The customary response to any religious grievance, real or imagined, was collective violence.

Some thought that the way to avoid the despair caused by competition for the limited work available was to hold back the flood of immigration. Nativist sentiments combined with religious antagonism in an attempt to exclude the masses waiting to immigrate to America, but to no avail. America and its fabled bounty remained a magnet to millions whose homeland afflictions blinded them to the reality of life on this new continent. In no small measure, the shipping companies had solicited passengers by promoting the vision of a welcoming, prosperous America, a message that was as persuasive (and as unrealistic) as any modern commercial advertising. This so-called "assisted immigration" was the remarkably successful product of the free enterprise system.

The United States was not unique in its internecine foundation, of course. Violence was — and remains — an international phenomenon. Yet, the uncertainty of life in America combined with the glorification of violence in popular myths left an indelible impression on all who would participate in this society. It should be no surprise that violence connected with America's national game mirrored this American reality.

Fanatics

Most attendees at nineteenth century baseball games were not out of control, and there are no reports of widespread homicides or bedlam. There was a general rowdiness, however, by men who were used to behaving in that manner. Throughout the history of the sport, efforts were made to attract women to the contests in the hope that their presence would pacify the crowds. Nineteenth century club owners created Ladies Day, offering free admission to any woman accompanying a man. The women, however, did little to dampen the disposition of the over-enthusiastic crowd. Although the women would not enter into the brawls, they eagerly joined in the gambling, baiting and hollering.

It is true that the nineteenth century baseball crowds were diverse. The Troy, New York newspaper noted that spectators at the baseball exhibitions included "judges, lawyers, bankers, doctors, clergymen, merchants, clerks, mechanics, students, railroad men, laborers, farmers, officials, editors, printers' devils, bootblacks, and so on, all anxious to see a good game." The *New York Sun* in 1884 remarked about

> the good nature, affability, and friendliness of the crowd. The slim schoolboy ten years of age, and the fat, lager-beer saloon proprietor of fifty talk gracefully about the game as it progresses as though they had known each other for years. Men exchange opinions freely about the game with persons they never saw before and everybody seems good natured and happy.

The *Sun* acknowledged that this "contentment" was disturbed when the umpire rendered an unfavorable ruling. "The good sense of the crowd," however, quickly settled "back into its accustomed condition."

Although rare, fans have attacked ballplayers away from the ball field. One troubled 19-year-old fan, Chicagoan Ruth Ann Steinhagen, had

Ruth Ann Steinhagen, obsessed with first baseman Eddie Waitkus, lured him to her hotel room and shot him in the chest, saying "If I can't have you, nobody could." Waitkus returned to baseball the following season, and Steinhagen was found criminally insane and committed to Kankakee State Hospital.

been obsessed with Cubs first baseman Eddie Waitkus for years. He was a journeyman, hardly a star. Steinhagen would attend Cubs games and wait by the players' gate after the game to catch sight of him. When Waitkus passed by, Steinhagen would shrink into a corner and tremble. She never spoke to him, but erected a shrine to him on her night table with pictures and newspaper clippings.

Prior to the 1949 season, Cubs dealt Waitkus to the Phillies, and Steinhagen was depressed after he left town. The Phillies traveled to Chicago in the middle of the 1949 season for a series against the Cubs. On June 14, 1949, young Miss Steinhagen checked into the Edgewater Beach Hotel, where the Phillies stayed, using the last name and address of a family Waitkus grew up with in Boston. Steinhagen had been at the ballpark that day watching the Phillies beat the Cubs, 9–2. She sent Waitkus a note inviting him up to her room (#1297-A): "Mr. Waitkus — It's extremely important that I see you as soon as possible. We're not acquainted, but I have something of importance to speak to you about." She gave a bellhop $5 to deliver the note, ordered a daiquiri and two whiskey sours from room service and waited. When Waitkus entered her room, she took a 22 caliber rifle out of the closet — she had smuggled it into the hotel in pieces wrapped in newspaper and reassembled it in her room. She told Waitkus to go to the window: "If I can't have you, nobody could." She then shot him in the chest.

Steinhagen called the front desk and told them what she had done. They rushed Waitkus to the hospital, and he survived. The bullet had just missed his heart and lodged near his spine. Police arrested Steinhagen and charged her with attempted murder. She "almost happily" confessed that she shot Waitkus for the "thrill. . . . I wanted to do away with him, that's all — to do something exciting in my life. I didn't want to go back to being a typist." She didn't. Doctors diagnosed her as insane — she had explained that "all of my dreams have come true"— and she spent three years in a mental institution. She claimed: "I have never been so happy in my life." Waitkus returned to baseball the following season and was named the Comeback Player of the Year. Bernard Malamud later popularized Steinhagen's gun attack on Waitkus in his classic novel of baseball and American life, *The Natural*.

Chicago was also the sight of an earlier fan shooting. Cabaret dancer Violet Popovich Valli shot Cubs shortstop Bill Jurges on the morning of July 6, 1932, at the Hotel Carlos, the summer home of many of the unmarried Cubs just two blocks from Wrigley Field. She was distraught with Jurges because their "beautiful" love affair had ended. She took a

.25 caliber revolver from her purse and threatened to kill herself. Jurges grabbed the gun and in the struggle three shots were fired. One hit Jurges in the chest, another in his left hand. A third hit Valli in the right wrist. Jurges and Valli recovered at the Illinois Masonic hospital, the same hospital Eddie Waitkus was brought to seventeen years later. Valli had left a note to the world in her apartment: "To me life without Billy isn't worth living, but why should I leave this life alone? I'm going to take Billy with me."

Jurges declined to prosecute, and when he recovered he continued his baseball career for another 15 seasons with the National League clubs in Chicago and New York. Valli took advantage of her fame, signing a 22-week contract to perform at Chicago nightclubs. In 1946 and 1947, Jurges played shortstop for the Cubs while Eddie Waitkus played first.

Modern Misbehavior

The ruffian conventions of the nineteenth century have also characterized modern baseball, but only on occasion. The most notorious recent examples took place at the home stadium of the Chicago White Sox on the South Side of Chicago. On the night of September 19, 2002, a shirtless and tattooed father-and-son team of miscreants, William Ligue Jr. and his 15-year-old boy Michael, jumped from behind first base and pummeled the 54-year-old Kansas City coach Tom Gamboa before they were removed from the field. Both pled guilty to criminal charges. Dad Ligue was sentenced to thirty months of probation and community service. He was ordered to attend classes on parenting, remain in a substance abuse program and follow a curfew for 90 days. The judge recommended that Son Ligue be sent to "prison boot camp." Coach Gamboa later commented: "I think people just have too much to drink." Gamboa suffered minor, but permanent, hearing loss in his right ear from the attack.

Seven months later at the same ballpark, a fan attacked first base umpire Laz Diaz at the end of the eighth inning. Diaz, a former Marine, quickly dispatched the delinquent: "The good hand-to-hand combat they taught me worked." Eric Dybas, 24 and drunk, was the fourth fan to run on to the field that night. He was charged with one count of felony aggravated battery and one count of misdemeanor criminal trespass. Dybas pled guilty and, clutching his paperback bible, was sentenced to six months in the Cook County jail.

Fans attacking players on the field are rarer in the modern game, but not unheard off. Wrigley Field installed a 42-inch steel-mesh screen to separate the bleacherites from the outfielders, but there was direct access to the field from other portions of the park. The last week of the 1995 season, the Cubs remained in contention for the playoffs. James Mouton of the Houston Astros homered off Cubs reliever Randy Myers. That apparently was the last straw for John Murray, a 27-year-old bond trader. He charged out of the right field stands and attacked Mouton as he circled the bases. Murray later explained: "I was watching the game with some friends and I told them if Myers gives up another homer to a guy I'm going to run out on the field and yell at him. In retrospect, it was a bad move on my part."

Jimmy Piersall was known to be a fine ballplayer, but afflicted with personal demons. While playing for the Cleveland Indians in 1961, Piersall was attacked by two fans who ran out of the right field stands at Yankee Stadium during the seventh inning of the first game of a doubleheader. Piersall later related what happened in the fight that ensued, the first one Piersall said he had ever won:

> They came at me like madmen, hurling insults. I could see fire in their eyes. One of them yelled, "We'll get you, you nut," and cocked his right hand to hit me. I didn't wait to hear any more. I got in the first punch. I got the first guy with a left hook, and he went down. I hit the other with a right, but the punch landed a little high on the temple and he stayed up. He tried to get away, but I connected with a kick in his rear before the cops grabbed him.

The police held the two teenagers on charges of disorderly conduct.

In addition to individual incidents of spectators intruding on the field, there have been some completely disgraceful occasions when an entire ballpark of fans has lost control. Management was certainly at fault in each instance, and beer seems to be the intoxicant of choice that unleashed the fan violence. In the summer of 1974, the Cleveland Indians hosted ten-cent beer night at Municipal Stadium. 25,000 fans consumed 60,000 servings of beers and, as might have been foreseen, they rioted. With the score tied 5–5 against the visiting Texas Rangers, the fans let loose in the ninth inning, running on the field, throwing chairs and punches. Fans hit umpire Nestor Chylak and Indians relief pitcher Tom Hilgendorf with chairs. Rangers manager Billy Martin grabbed a bat and cried, "Let's get 'em, boys!" His players kept Martin from doing any damage. Police escorted both teams out of the park, and the umpires awarded the Rangers a 9–0 forfeit victory.

Equally bizarre was the July 13, 1979, celebration of Disco Night at Comiskey Park in Chicago. Admission was 98 cents for those fans who brought a disco record. Some 49,000 attended. Between games of the White Sox-Tigers doubleheader, management stuffed the records into a large wooden container and blew it up. Thousands of fans rioted. They brawled on the field and set bonfires with the debris. At least one suit was filed seeking $700,000 for a hip injury that resulted when an intoxicated man fell on the plaintiff from the upper deck during the rampage. "These weren't real baseball fans," said White Sox owner Bill Veeck. "All I know is we won't try anything like this again. I was amazed. I wish I wasn't."

Sometimes the debris hurled at players from the stands to the field can be frightful. On August 26, 1986, a Yankee Stadium fan threw a Bowie hunting knife with a five-inch blade at California Angels rookie Wally Joyner after the home team suffered a 2–0 loss. The knife's butt end just grazed Joyner, causing no injury: "This is crazy; it's unbelievable. I am glad we don't have to come back here." No suspects were apprehended.

Playing in the Oakland Coliseum on April 19, 2003, Texas Rangers outfielder Carl Everett was hit on the head by a cell phone thrown from the second deck by Juan-Carlos Covarrubias-Serrano, 24, of Palo Alto, who was drunk. Police charged the reprobate with assault with a deadly weapon. Everett commented: "This crowd has always been surly. They throw stuff all the time." (Everett was correct. In 2001, the Oakland Coliseum's right field crowd had thrown coins and ice cubes at Seattle's splendid outfielder Ichiro Suzuki.) A few days later, an Oakland police officer nearly had his finger bitten off during an A's game. As a result of these two incidents in the same week, the club changed its policy that had allowed the sale of beer up to an hour after the end of the game. Thereafter, service would stop at the seventh inning.

Sometimes the detritus flowing from the stands has been more traditional, although equally dangerous. In 1940, the *Sporting News* editorialized in favor of the "elimination of the deadly pop bottle." There were good historical reasons for that concern. On July 8, 1907, fans bombarded Cubs manager Frank Chance with soda bottles throughout a game in Brooklyn. Finally, he threw one bottle back in the stands. It hit a young boy and cut his leg. The fans rushed to surround Chance, who left the field in an armored car with a police escort.

Ebbets Field was also the site of an onslaught of bottle throwing so dense it was referred to as "Flatbush confetti." On May 22, 1921, the fans were so upset by the calls of the umpire Cy Rigler that they showered pop bottles in his direction, but none reached its mark. This "most shameful demonstration of rowdyism," according to the *New York Times*, did not help the Brooklyn Robins, who lost the contest in twelve innings.

After Joe "Ducky" Medwick slid hard into Detroit's third baseman Marvin Owen, fans at the seventh game of the 1934 World Series heaved pop bottles, oranges, apples and tomatoes at the Cardinal's left fielder. They conveniently ignored the fact that Owen had started the fracas by intentionally stepping on Medwick's leg before the Cardinal star kicked back. Perhaps they were simply frustrated by the fact that the game stood 9–0 at that point against the hometown Tigers and that Owen had no hits in his last twelve at bats in the series. (He would add to his infamous record by going hitless in his first 19 times at bat in the 1936 series, a record of futility that still stands.)

When Medwick proceeded to his outfield position, the vegetables, fruit and glassware onslaught increased. The *Chicago Tribune* reported: "The shower continued, so Medwick backed up to the infield while groundskeepers harvested the debris." Commissioner Landis, in attendance for the fall classic, turned umpire himself and ordered Medwick off the field to keep the fans from rioting. Landis later said he could not blame the crowd, because he too had been upset with Medwick for retaliating. With Dizzy Dean on the mound, the Cardinals won the game anyway, 11–0, and triumphed in the hard-fought series four games to three.

At times, it has been the ballplayers who have totally lost control at the boundary line between the field and the stands. Perhaps the most notorious recent incident occurred on May 16, 2000, when members of the Los Angeles Dodgers entered the stands at Chicago's Wrigley Field after a drunken spectator had reached into the bullpen and assaulted backup catcher Chad Kreuter. Kreuter entered the stands with a half dozen other Dodgers to follow, trading punches with fans. The Commissioner suspended 16 players and three coaches for a total of 76 games, the most in baseball history from a single incident. Three fans were charged with disorderly conduct, and the Cubs increased security in the bullpen area. Kreuter served an eight-game suspension and paid a $5,000 fine.

One final example will suffice. On September 13, 2004, during the ninth inning of a game between the visiting Texas Rangers and the homestanding Oakland Athletics, Rangers relief pitcher Frank Francisco threw a chair that hit 41-year-old fan Jennifer Bueno. The chair broke her nose. Ranger manager Bucky Showalter later said that the fan's language had gone "way over the line." Apparently, the Rangers had experienced similar problems on prior visits to Oakland. Francisco was taken from the stadium directly to jail where he was booked and fingerprinted. The next morning he was charged with aggravated battery, later reduced to a misdemeanor assault.

Commissioner Bud Selig pleaded that the players must exercise more restraint: "Listen, this has gone on 100 years," referring to the heckling. "It's gone on at Ebbets Field and a lot of other places. You have to learn not to listen to that stuff or react to it." Selig then suspended Francisco for the remainder of the 2004 season. On June 30, 2005, Francisco pled no contest to the criminal charge and an Alameda County Superior Court judge sentenced him to 179 days in the county jail. All but 30 days were suspended, and he was allowed to serve that time in a work-release program in Texas. He was also ordered to pay Ms. Bueno's medical bills, complete an anger management program and serve 500 hours in the community. Francisco returned to the Rangers' major league roster in September 2006 and appeared in eight games.

Fortunately, these examples of outrageous conduct by players and fans have not prompted an onslaught of attention-seeking copycats. Players know that irresponsible action will result in stiff fines, suspensions and even criminal charges. In general, baseball fans either appreciate their proper place in the entertainment spectacle or are deterred by security. They have paid their fare to watch, to cheer, to boo, but not to participate in the contest on the field.

Kill the Ump

"Most baseball fans," said the great Christy Mathewson, "look upon an umpire as a sort of necessary evil to the luxury of baseball, like the odor that follows an automobile." Nineteenth century umpires were in a particularly dangerous position, especially when the crowd had placed bets on the outcome of the contests. As the single sentinel of neutrality on a field of partisans surrounded by a crowd of home team rooters, the sole umpire — most games in the nineteenth century used only one umpire — would often suffer verbal and, at times, physical abuse.

On August 23, 1860, the great rivalry between Brooklyn's two major amateur clubs, the Atlantics and the Excelsiors, brought a crowd of 20,000 to a neutral site, Brooklyn's Putnam Base Ball Club grounds. It was the third and deciding game of their championship series. Spectators heavily favored the Atlantics and heaped vile abuse on their rivals. The clubs selected Mr. Henry Thorn of the Empire Club as their neutral umpire. Early in the contest, an Atlantics player balked at the umpire's call, and later the *Brooklyn Eagle* reported that the pro-Atlantic cranks joined in with "insulting epithets and loud comments on the decision of the umpire." The crowd, according to the *New York Times*, became "unsupportable in its violence," and began shouting for a new umpire. A hundred policemen attempted to restore order, but without much success. Excelsior captain James Leggett, justifiably concerned for the safety of his boys, pulled his club off the field and left the grounds, pummeled with stones by the mob that followed the escaping players.

The next day the local newspapers excoriated the crowd for its "disgraceful" misbehavior, suggesting that gambling was the root cause of the disruption. The *Brooklyn Eagle* worried that "a little further decadence will reduce the attendance at ball matches to the level of the prize ring and the race course." The *New York Times* applauded the action of the Excelsior club that avoided further bloodshed as "worthy of great praise," meeting "the approval of the vast majority of the respectable portion of the base ball community." It explained that the game was "drawn, and, if ever played out, will take place in comparative privacy, on some enclosed ground."

In 1886, the *Atlanta Constitution* printed in full the common ditty about the fate of the umpire:

> Mother, may I slug the umpire?
> May I slug him right away?
> So he cannot be there, mother
> When the clubs begin to play?
> Let me clasp his throat, dear mother
> In a dear delightful grip
> With one hand, and with the other
> Bat him several in the lip.
> Let me climb his frame, dear mother
> While the happy people shout;
> I'll not kill him, dearest mother —
> I will only knock him out.

Let me mop the ground up, mother
With his person, dearest do;
If the ground can stand it, mother,
I don't see why you can't too.
Mother, may I slug the umpire —
Slug him right between the eyes;
If you'll let me do it, mother,
You shall have the champion prize.

It is surprising that more incidents did not occur, especially when gambling money was at stake. It was not until 1912 that the major leagues required two umpires to cover each game. Three-man crews were first used in the regular season in 1933, and four-man crews became standard in both leagues in 1952.

Life did not improve much for umpires in the twentieth century. St. Louis fans beat up the National League's best umpire, Hank O'Day, in 1901. O'Day needed a police escort to escape the park. In 1906, a bottle thrown from the stands in St. Louis hit umpire Billy Evans, only 22 years old and a rookie arbiter behind the plate. The attack fractured his skull. By that winter, he was back in shape and, according to the *Washington Post*, umpiring five nights a week in the Ohio Polo League. The *Post* still expressed doubts about the quality of his work on the ball field: "Bill may be a rattling good roller polo official, but on the diamond, well —."

American League umpire Emmett "Red" Ormsby suffered a concussion in 1929 when struck on the head by a pop bottle thrown by a fan while Ormsby was officiating at third base in a game in Cleveland between the Indians and the Philadelphia Athletics. Semi-conscious, he was helped off the field. This was the second such incident at Dunn Field in Cleveland that season, and the President of the American League, E. S. Barnard, suspended Cleveland skipper Roger Peckinpaugh for five days for inciting the fans.

On September 16, 1940, after a Leo Durocher tantrum at Ebbets Field, a fan punched umpire George Magerkurth. (There is some evidence that this was intended as a diversion so the attacker's associate could pickpocket the crowd.) Magerkurth was no angel, however. While still a minor league umpire, he was once arrested for fighting with a player under the stands. Another time, he was suspended for spitting at a player. After the Dodgers won the 1941 pennant, the victory parade down Fulton Street included a coffin labeled "Magerkurth."

American League umpire Joe Rue summarized his decade in blue:

> I've been mobbed, cussed, booed, kicked in the ass, punched in the face, hit with mud balls and whiskey bottles, and had everything from shoes to fruits and vegetables thrown at me. I've been hospitalized with a concussion and broken ribs. I've been spit on and soaked with lime and water. I've probably experienced more violence than any other umpire who lived.

Other umpires would contest Rue's claim to supremacy.

The common ballpark caution not to "kill the umpire" was only marginally hyperbolic. Johnny Evers, the scrappy Chicago Cubs Hall of Famer stated what many players thought privately: "My favorite umpire is a dead one." Many umpires had to be escorted from the field to avoid grievous injury at the hands of the cranks. Some umpires fought back.

Umpire Tim Hurst was hired by the National League in 1891. Raised in coal mining country in Pennsylvania, Hurst knew how to mix it up with his fists. (He also refereed boxing matches in the off-season.) When ballplayers disputed his calls, sometimes a punch was thrown — by Hurst! Other times Hurst would respond verbally. Mike Donlin, a National League outfielder, told a story about the time Hurst called a strike on a pitch to him and Donlin beefed. Hurst called the next pitch a ball. Donlin turned to Hurst and said: "Why Tim, that was better than the one you called a strike." "Is that so?" Hurst replied. "Well, then it's two strikes and not one."

Umpires like Hurst shared an arrogance borne of their isolation, but, in large measure, no one questioned their honesty. They loved to perform, even before a hostile crowd. Hurst enjoyed recalling a game he umpired on August 4, 1897, in Cincinnati when a disgruntled spectator hurled a beer stein out of the stands, striking him on the back. Hurst gave as good as he got — he once invaded the grandstand in Cincinnati and broke a fan's nose with his mask.

An umpire's calls had to be instantaneous and correct. In any case, they were final and binding. Tommy Connolly, a long time umpire, described his career: "Maybe I called it wrong, but it's official." It was Connolly who was umpiring at home plate in the Polo Grounds the day in 1920 that Carl Mays' submarine pitch killed Ray Chapman.

Heckling and Brutality

Even Mickey Mantle, the great Yankee, was booed on occasion: "I don't care who you are," he told *Look Magazine* in 1969, "you hear those boos." Babe Ruth explained to a group of schoolboys in 1929 how he planned to deal with hecklers in right field:

> If any fan in the future uses indecent language, either to me or any other Yankee, I will stop the game, call a policeman, and have the fan thrown out of the park. I am going to be my own law from now on.

Most major leaguers take heckling in stride, but not every ballplayer has been able to ignore the taunting of the fans. None did it better, however, than Bruce Hurst, the fine pitcher for the Red Sox and the Padres in the 1980s and early 1990s. When verbally attacked, Hurst, who did not curse, would simply respond: "Oh, go wash your car!" Shoeless Joe Jackson reportedly responded to a Cleveland heckler, who kept asking him if he knew how to spell "illiterate," by hitting a triple and then asking: "Hey, big mouth, how you spell triple?"

Most spectators played baseball as youngsters. Watching the professional players at work, they naturally think they could do a better job and at less money. They are not shy about letting the players know their feelings. Pittsburgh manager Danny Murtagh's attitude seems to reflect the views of most ballplayers:

Why certainly I'd like to have that fellow who hits a home run every time at bat, who strikes out every opposing batter when he's pitching, who throws strikes to any base or the plate when he's playing outfield and who's always thinking about two innings ahead just what he'll do to baffle the other team. Any manager would want a guy like that playing for him. The only trouble is to get him to put down his cup of beer and come down out of the stands and do those things.

A Violent Society

Baseball violence on the field and at the park mirrored daily American life. Although some today seem to wish for a society where everyone can pack his or her own concealed weapon, our unique American experience has shown that armament does not deter violence, but only makes it a more readily available option. Even before we had guns for everyone, there were sticks and bricks. Now anyone can carry the means to instantly extinguish the lives of others.

American history is besmirched by violent episodes, some orchestrated by various layers of government, others by private gangs. Until fairly recently, lynching was a way of life or death for African Americans who were thought to have stepped beyond their social station. Government troops regularly quelled peaceful labor protests with gunfire. In 1915, the Texas Rangers (the troopers, not the baseball team) murdered hundreds of innocent Mexican-Americans. The government's war of extermination against the Indians lasted for decades.

Private violence with public complicity and acceptance ranged widely over American history. The Bowery Boys Riot of 1857 in lower New York City pitted nativists against immigrants. Klan members assassinated civil rights workers. Private armies crushed unionists. Dead opponents could cause little trouble.

What we have seen in baseball on occasion is a tamed version of the anarchy that frequently characterized American society. Fist fights and pushing matches are not gun play and knifings, but the willingness to pursue violence as a first option is part of American life and baseball history. The National Game may not be as intentionally violent as football, our other national sports obsession, but it has never been a tea party.

Baseball Commissioner Bart Giamatti refused to allow Pete Rose
to degrade the "historical enterprise" of the National Game.

Conclusion:
Work, Play and Betrayal

The strongest thing baseball has going for it today is its yesterdays.
— Lawrence Ritter

IN THE SECOND HALF OF THE NINETEENTH CENTURY, baseball quickly achieved the status of an affordable entertainment for those who wanted to watch the best players perform at the highest levels of athletic excellence. It was played in the growing urban centers as well as smaller cities across the country. For professional ballplayers, of course, the game was both work and play. Although baseball was an occupation riddled with uncertainty and always shorter in duration than a typical working lifetime, the game offered countervailing benefits. Baseball afforded a few talented young men the opportunity to earn a good income doing something they loved to do. Although men and women regularly complain about their jobs, few baseball players regret their lives in the game.

Many adults remember fondly their own adolescent days playing America's game. We could (and did) dream of playing baseball at the major league level, but participation in the summer's pastime was fun at any level. Many continued to play the game, at least in its softball variation, throughout their adult years. Baseball is a favored form of play across boundaries of class, race and education.

Because we knew the game through personal experience, Americans have always had trouble understanding how baseball could be anything other than sport, a lark, an amusement. Albert Spalding wrote in 1907: "The average Base Ball enthusiast cares little or nothing for the business side of the game and is inclined to resent any effort to place it before him." Even when ballplayer wages were held down by collusion among the magnates — the state of affairs for the first century of the professional game — the fortunate athletes who played at the major league level were always paid much higher salaries than other working men and women. Today, they are paid higher salaries than CEOs. And they earn those salaries by playing a children's game for our entertainment. Many other entertainers, such as actors, who are also well compensated, seem to have to work at their craft. For professional ballplayers at the highest level, the game seems easy to play. How can play be work?

America has always been torn between the Calvinist ethos of hard work and the Continental approval of frivolous play. The *New York Sun* editorialized about this conflict around the turn of the twentieth century and explained the connection between work and play:

> Work is as essential to the well being of the mind as it is to the maintenance of the body; and he who thinks he can live without it does not know what the effect of trying the experiment would be. The pleasure of rest, for instance, is entirely dependent upon work. Without fatigue, repose affords no enjoyment.... But more than this, there is in good hard work an intrinsic pleasure which every one can have if he will, without waiting for rest, amusement or any other reward.

Hard work, self-sacrifice and self-discipline were always part of the prevailing morality of America. Gambling, frivolity, and handouts were not American, or were they? Americans saw themselves as a sober, driven, Christian people. A society devoid of restraints was dangerous. What then was baseball? How did it reflect America's definition of itself? Was it work? Was it play? The game starts when the umpire chants: "Play ball!" No one says: "Work ball," except George Will in his exceptional baseball book *Men at Work.*

Hugh Fullerton, writing in the *North American Review* in 1930, suggested the following ad be placed for major leaguers:

> Big pay, short hours, easy work, mostly play. Loaf half the year. All expenses paid while traveling. Jobs always open for right men.

Fullerton yearned for the good old days when players were paid more modest salaries, when the game was "rough, rowdy and rugged."

He was concerned that the game had gone soft. How could these base-ball players leave the game wealthy in exchange for simply having "fun?"

The Glorious Past

Red Sox guru pitcher Bill Lee told the *Los Angeles Times* in 1977: "Base-ball is the belly button of our society." Although he did not explain — "Spaceman" Lee rarely explained — perhaps he meant that baseball con-nects us to the umbilical cord of our own history. It is the point that ties the generations together. It is part of our genes. It is the nexus of the conversation that always takes place within our community. As Connie Mack said in 1951 as he neared the end of a lifetime in the National Game: "No matter what I talk about, I always get back to baseball." So it seems for many in society.

The confusion of play and work in the National Game, however, speaks to a fundamental disorientation in American life. This is a coun-try where due diligence was needed to reap the benefits of honest labor, but where a class made wealthy through inheritance could "play" un-abated. Without titles of royalty, we preserved the prerogatives of titles. Although always a tiny minority, the elite have maintained their social, economic and political control throughout our history.

Baseball, however, remains above the quotidian civil fray. When pol-itics are too divisive and life's allocation of assets remain unfair, we can always turn to the league standings and to our rivalries on the diamond for controversy without real consequences. "Whatever else it is," said fel-low entertainer Lillian Russell, "the game is wholesome." More people attend major league baseball games each year than any other profes-sional sport. We revere the players, because they represent all that hu-mankind can be physically. We treasure the game, even when sometimes it makes us care too much and we are almost always disappointed with the ultimate outcome of each season.

As we have seen, the game is also crooked and nasty. We accept these impurities as part of the package. We will accept anything but betrayal. Perhaps that is why the performance-enhancing drug scandal in baseball bothers us so much. If we think that ballplayers' performances are simply the product of a bottle or a syringe, they are no longer worthy of our emulation or adulation.

What lessons can we learn from the National Game? A baseball player who is successful at bat one time out of three is considered a superstar. Might our work lives have similar odds! If we made two mistakes for every good decision, we would not last long in the trade. Each strikeout hurts, but we know that each player will get at least three at-bats a game before the day is through.

The notables of the game have always opined on the lessons baseball teaches to the next generation. The *Spalding Guide* of 1912 boasted:

> A game which teaches fair play and honorable effort to the growing generation is building a national character which will establish itself for good around the world. The more of it, the better. [There is a] growing tendency to decry victory at any cost for the better rule of victory earned in a thoroughly sportsmanlike manner.

Do we actually care about sportsmanship in losers? What should we think of a game which teaches cheating and dishonorable efforts, glorifies violence and has long countenanced the use of performance-enhancing substances, a game that values winning and only winning? "Wait 'til next year," remember, was the cry of losers, not the prediction of the winners who expected to repeat the following season.

Spalding's *Guide* lauded America's "spirit of fairness" that "impelled them to demand of the players that they play strictly on their merits and not attempt to win by intimidation or by the use of methods which were once considered 'smart,' but which are lacking in sterling purity." This puffing by baseball's most prolific apostle is belied by the facts. Pitchers won through intimidation, sign stealers prevailed by methods that lacked "sterling purity," and the mighty home run hitters cashed in on their muscle rather than on their morals. It has always been so. In 1912, the celebrated Ty Cobb took exception to Boston pitcher Dutch Leonard's inside fastballs:

So I dragged a bunt which their first baseman was forced to field, Leonard ran to first to take the throw. When he saw I was going for him and not the bag, he kept on running into the coaching box. Damned coward. I ignored the bag, drove right through after him.

The reality and the invention collided. We can see it more easily in our game than in our daily lives.

Giamatti and Rose

Commissioner A. Bartlett Giamatti understood the role of baseball in the American galaxy. During his too brief turn at bat as the leader of the National Game, the former classics professor and president of Yale University brought a distinguished élan to his office. What other chief executive would say, upon accepting the commissioner's position, "Dante would have been delighted?" (Most would ask whether Dante was that guy who used to play third base for the Phillies.) Giamatti knew that he and his fellow eminences were simply "temporary custodians of an enduring public trust." He appreciated the importance of the game to the people who came to watch it or followed it in the media:

> The largest thing I've learned is that enormous grip that this game has on people, the extent to which it really is very important. It goes way down deep. It really does bind together. It's a cliché and sounds sentimental, but I have now seen it from the inside....I think I underestimated the depth of this historical enterprise.

Giamatti could wax eloquently on the glories of the game, but he was realistic when it came to the dark side of the diamond. He banned Pete Rose from the pantheon of the sport's heroes, because "one of the game's greatest players has engaged in a variety of acts which have stained the game, and he must now live with the consequences of those acts." Rose had betrayed the game. Giamatti's successor Fay Vincent would be less mellifluent: "Pete Rose was a vicious, and I think some-what demented, person, and I think he still is."

Pete Rose was baseball's most prolific hitter. He loved his life's work, once saying "I'd walk through hell in a gasoline suit to play baseball." He also gambled on baseball games while he was manager of his hometown Cincinnati Reds, including games involving the Reds. There may be some alternative explanation for the betting slips in Rose's handwriting collected by New York City lawyer John Dowd in his investigation for Major League Baseball, but a contrary inference is really hard to imagine. Although Rose was a great hero for many youngsters and was truly beloved in the Queen City, the documented evidence of his wrongdoing was compelling.

What exactly was Rose's transgression? There is no question that Rose violated Major League Rule 21(d) that is posted in every clubhouse: "Any player, umpire, or club or league official or employee, who shall bet any sum whatsoever upon any baseball game in connection with which the bettor has a duty to perform shall be declared permanently ineligible." No one has suggested, however, and they could not prove it, that Rose acted any differently as the manager of the Reds during those games in which he had a direct gambling stake, as compared with those games in which he had none.

Rose's gambling behavior sent a message to those who had knowledge of his bets. Bookies, gamblers and the mob knew when it was a propitious time to place a bet on the Reds and when it might be best to pass. If the club's manager was unwilling to risk his money, why would others? If the club's manager put his money on the line, shouldn't they join him in the wager?

Giamatti's commissioner's office recognized in light of the unsavory history of gambling in the game that Rose's impropriety was potentially devastating to the baseball business. Faced with compelling evidence of his involvement in gambling and hounded by the federal government on tax evasion charges related to cash payments for his signature on sports memorabilia, Rose accepted Giamatti's suspension without acknowledging any fault. In fact, Rose denied for more than a decade what was obvious to anyone who read the publicly available Dowd report. Rose betrayed his sport. Rose had a serious problem with gambling, far beyond the compulsions of the occasional casino visitor. His repeated public denials in the face of overwhelming objective evidence were a telling indication that Rose was a pathological gambler.

In his recent autobiography, *My Prison Without Bars*, Rose moved closer to acknowledging the full extent of his illness, but characteristically he blamed others: "If I had been an alcoholic or a drug addict, baseball would have suspended me for six weeks and paid for my rehabilitation...but baseball had no fancy rehab for gamblers like they do for drug addicts."

Pathological gambling is a progressive, chronic disease, but it can be successfully arrested through treatment and impulse control. In fact, Rose has sought treatment. Physicians and psychologists who diagnose and treat compulsive gambling examine patient behaviors that present gambling as an escape from a reality that a patient is either unable or unwilling to accept. Compulsive gamblers often suffer from severe mood swings and depression, emotional insecurity and immaturity when away from the action. Dr. Joseph Zieleniewski, a sports psychologist, explained to The *Sporting News* in 1991: "Generally speaking, athletes need excitement. They are sensation-seeking persons. They can become depressed when they aren't thrill-seeking." In effect, gambling becomes a form of therapy for their depression.

The lure of gambling is ever-present in American society. Estimates are that up to 70 percent of the population participates in some form of gambling every year. Very few — perhaps three percent — do so to an extent that they might be diagnosed as pathological gamblers.

If we recognize that Rose, the great ballplayer, suffered from an addiction, was suspension from the game the correct sanction for his behavior? It seems appropriate to draw a distinction between Rose's place in baseball history and any continuing role he might have in the business of baseball in any capacity. Rose is correct that an alcoholic would not be punished for his addiction, but he also would not be placed in charge of a large organization if his condition would interfere with the performance of his responsibilities. Any request to return Rose to the bench in Cincinnati (or anywhere else) would rightfully be denied. It is true that a recovering alcoholic or drug addict may be able to function fully in society, but there are always risks associated with their conditions. The risk of gambling, especially when with new technology that can be accomplished from a laptop without any need for a "runner" to carry wagers from the dugout to a bookie, are too significant to ignore.

Thus, for most fans the tragedy of Pete Rose has narrowed down to the debate whether he should ever be allowed to be considered for election to baseball's Hall of Fame. There can be little doubt that, were it not for his involvement with bookies, Pete Rose would have been voted into the Hall on the first ballot in the fifth year after he completed his career as a player. His performance on the diamond was unrivaled. Over 24 seasons as a player, almost all with the Cincinnati Reds and the Philadelphia Phillies, Rose accumulated more hits, had more at bats and played in more games than any other player in the history of the sport. Who can gainsay that his career warranted Hall of Fame recognition?

There is also good reason to believe that Commissioner Giamatti did not intend that Rose be kept out of the Hall. Giamatti did nothing to change the Hall's eligibility rules, which, at the time of the suspension, did not speak to the issue whether a person had to be on baseball's eligible list to stand for election. He said: "When Pete Rose is eligible" after the normal waiting period, the Baseball Writers Association of America "will count the ballots and decide whether he belongs in the Hall of Fame."

Yet the doubters contend that Rose's gambling should disqualify him from eligibility for the Hall. Others respond that many inductees to the Hall had blemishes on their personal records. Babe Ruth, Ty Cobb, Tris Speaker, Leo Durocher, Eddie Collins, Ray Schalk, Rube Waddell, Joe DiMaggio, and Mickey Mantle — to name only a few — were not spiritual beings. Some were as addicted to gambling as Rose. Some even publicly gambled on contests in which they participated. For example, in 1905 Giants manager John McGraw publicly bet on the World Series

games in which his Giants performed. There is no clear evidence, however, that any of the enshrined stars, including McGraw, gambled day-in
and day-out on baseball games the way Rose did.

Is it possible to draw a line between a player's personal off-field life
and his public on-field life? Babe Ruth was a dreadful role model off the
field. On the field, however, Ruth was a model of appropriate excess,
swatting home runs and helping the Yankees win ballgames. We should
not censure Pete Rose for what he did off the field. However, his misconduct while managing baseball games was of a different order.

If we understand compulsive gambling for what it is — an illness like
other addictions — the answer to the Rose controversy becomes clearer.
He should not be excommunicated for his illness. Rose earned recognition for his splendid career on the field. The Hall is filled with players
who suffered from serious personality defects, and yet they were honored for their remarkable baseball careers. Eventually, Pete Rose should
be honored in the same way and allowed to join his fellow baseball
greats in baseball's Hall of Fame.

Addressing the Illnesses of the Game

At times, baseball's dark side appears cancerous, ready to consume our
favorite pastime. Today with steroids, yesterday with intractable labor
disputes, and before that with alcohol and gambling, baseball has proven
itself impure and impious. We may rightfully scorn its transgressions,
but the game always seems to come back to thrill and entertain us.

We are left with a sport that is so much like the country in which it
thrives. We are a boastful people and claim more than can be justified.
We are an accomplished people, proud and effusive. Our game is much
the same. We take a game created and played domestically and term its
annual winner the World Champions. So much for humility.

There are those who would cleanse the game and American society
of those who do not fit the imagined model of propriety. Once the
major league game excluded black Americans, a testament to the mean-
spirited, bigoted nature of the nation. Now and again, some behavior,

such as drug use, warrants our public indignation, and for good reason. In other instances, good reason steps aside in the throes of passion.

Baseball does not need to be cured. The historical enterprise needs simply to be enjoyed as part of a full life in America, the game in all its glories and with all its vices. Like anything else, we can take our passion for the game too far, but, for the most part, baseball has fulfilled its early promise to become "a great national institution," as *The Spirit of the Times* wrote in 1857. As Henry Chadwick wrote in a letter to the *New York Times* in 1881, "the halcyon days of baseball are those of the present day." We have enjoyed that "present day" for 150 years. Bart Giamatti summed up, as follows:

> Baseball is not simply an essential part of this country, it is a living memory of what the American culture at its best works to be. Baseball is about going home, and how hard it is to get there, and how driven is our need. It tells us how good home is. Its wisdom says you can go home again, but that you cannot stay. The journey must always start once more until there is an ending to all journeying.

Notes

Researching baseball and American history has changed dramatically in the last decade. Historical newspapers and magazines are now available for search on-line through websites such as ProQuest.com. Google.com has begun to scan books out of copyright. In addition, libraries, such as the Baseball Hall of Fame in Cooperstown and the Boston Public Library, make historical documents easily accessible for researchers.

As always, the volumes of Harold Seymour's groundbreaking work, *Baseball: The Early Years*, and *Baseball: The Golden Age* offer the best place to start research into baseball history. The recent two volume work by Peter Morris, *A Game of Inches: The Stories Behind the Innovations that Shaped Baseball*, are now the definitive source on early baseball. Albert Spalding's *America's National Game* presents an interesting contemporary tract by one of the founders of the baseball business. Almost every major figure in baseball history discussed in this book has now been the subject of a well-researched biography, including John McGraw, Honus Wagner, Ty Cobb, Babe Ruth, Hal Chase and Cy Young. The internet also offers an abundance of the information in a variety of websites, a resource that will only increase over time. Sources for particular quotes are cited in the text.

Introduction
The *New York Times* covered the dinner at Delmonico's quite extensively. Cap Anson documented his own racism in his autobiography, *A Ball Player's Career*.

Chapter 1
The great Fashion Race Course tournament and the early days of the National Game were covered by newspapers and magazines of the time.

Chapter 2
Tom Melville's *Early Baseball and the Rise of the National League* provides a learned and thoughtful review of the game before 1880. John C. Burnham's book, *Bad Habits: Drinking, Smoking, Taking Drugs, Gambling, Sexual Misbehavior, and Swearing in American History* offers a most valuable overview of American vices. There

is also extensive literature on gambling in America, in particular how it affects sports. Daniel E. Ginsburg's *The Fix Is In: A History of Baseball Gambling and Game Fixing Scandals*, is the best source.

Chapter 3

David Q. Voigt's *American Baseball: From a Gentlemen's Sport to the Commissioner System*, tells the story of the Louisville caper. Other very useful sources on game-fixing in baseball include Steven A. Riess's *Major Problems in American Sport History* and David Callahan's *The Cheating Culture*. Matthew Josephson's *The Robber Barons* remains a fundamental work on American business in the Gilded Age, although Jack Beatty's new *Age of Betrayal: The Triumph of Money in America, 1865–1900* will certainly take its place as the definitive work. John Steele Gordon, *An Empire of Wealth: The Epic History of American Economic Power* and Harvey Wasserman's *History of the United States* also provide perspective.

The Black Sox scandal is discussed by David Pietrusza in his fine new book *Rothstein: The Life, Times and Murder of the Criminal Genius Who Fixed the 1919 World Series*. Errors in Eliot Asinov's well-known *Eight Men Out: The Black Sox and the 1919 World Series* have now been corrected in Gene Carney's *Burying the Black Sox: How Baseball's Cover-Up of the 1919 World Series Fix Almost Succeeded*.

Chapter 4

Alcoholism and drug abuse are discussed in a series of contemporary essays edited by Rebecca Shannonhouse, *Under the Influence: The Literature of Addiction*. Andrew Barr's *Drink: A Social History of America* was particularly valuable as was Mark Lender's and James Kirby's *Drinking in America*.

Brown-Séquard's elixir of life and its use by baseball players was discussed in contemporary newspaper articles.

Chapter 5

Violence on the diamond is discussed in Eric Dunning's *Sport Matters: Sociological Studies of Sports, Violence and Civilization*. Mike Sowell's *The Pitch That Killed* is a splendid source on the tragic death of Ray Chapman. There is also a rich literature on violence in society including Elizabeth Kandel Englander's *Understanding Violence*.

Chapter 6

Ty Cobb is the prime exemplar of dysfunctional violence in the National Game both on and off the field and Al Stump's *Cobb: A Biography* remains the definitive work on the life of the Georgia Peach. *Violence in America*, a three volume encyclopedia edited by Ronald Gottesman, is a comprehensive work.

Conclusion

James Reston's dual biography of Pete Rose and Bart Giamatti is a splendid source. *Collision at Home Plate: The Lives of Pete Rose and Bart Giamatti*. Pete Rose's *My Prison Without Bars* offers the ballplayer's take on his own travails.

Bibliography

Mikal Aasved, *The Psychodynamics and Psychology of Gambling*. Charles C. Thomas, Springfield, IL, 2002.

Roger I. Abrams, *Legal Bases: Baseball and the Law*. Temple University Press, Philadelphia, 1998.

Roger I. Abrams, *The Money Pitch: Baseball Free Agency and Salary Arbitration*. Temple University Press, Philadelphia, 2000.

Roger I. Abrams, *The First World Series and the Baseball Fanatics of 1903*. Northeastern University Press, Boston, 2003.

Kenneth D. Ackerman, *Boss Tweed: The Rise and Fall of the Corrupt Pol Who Conceived the Soul of Modern New York*. Carroll & Graf, New York, 2005.

Charles C. Alexander, *Ty Cobb*. Oxford University Press, New York, 1984.

Charles C. Alexander, *John McGraw*. University of Nebraska Press, Lincoln, Nebraska, 1988.

Charles C. Alexander, *Rogers Hornsby: A Biography*. Henry Holt and Co., New York, 1995.

Tyler Anbinder, *Five Points: The 19th Century New York City Neighborhood that Invented Tap Dance, Stole Elections, and Became the World's Most Notorious Slum*. Penguin, New York, 2001.

Roger Angell, *Game Time: A Baseball Companion*. Harcourt, Inc., New York, 2003.

Herbert Asbury, *Sucker's Progress: An Informal History of Gambling in America*. Thunder Mouth Press, New York, 1938.

Eliot Asinov, *Eight Men Out: The Black Sox and the 1919 World Series*. Owl Books, New York, 2000.

Richard Bak, *Peach: Ty Cobb in His Time and Ours*. Sports Media Group, Ann Arbor, 2005.

Andrew Barr, *Drink: A Social History of America*. Carroll & Graf Publishers, Inc., New York, 1999.

Gunther Barth, *City People: The Rise of Modern City Culture in Nineteenth-Century America*. Oxford University Press, New York, 1980.

Jack Beatty, *Age of Betrayal: The Triumph of Money in America, 1865–1900*. Alfred A. Knopf, New York, 2007.

David Block, *Baseball Before We Knew It: A Search for the Roots of the Game*. University of Nebraska Press, Lincoln, Nebraska, 2005.

Daniel J. Boorstin, *American Civilization*. McGraw-Hill Book Co., New York, 1972.

Eric Bronson, *Baseball and Philosophy: Thinking Outside the Batter's Box*. Open Court, Chicago, 2004.

Reed Browning, *Cy Young: A Baseball Life*. University of Massachusetts Press, Amherst, MA, 2000.

John C. Burnham, *Bad Habits: Drinking, Smoking, Taking Drugs, Gambling, Sexual Misbehavior, and Swearing in American History*. New York University Press, New York, 1991.

David Callahan, *The Cheating Culture*. Harcourt, Inc., New York, 2004.

Alexander B. Callow, Jr., *The Tweed Ring*. Oxford University Press, New York, 1965.

Jose Canseco, *Juiced: Wild Times, Rampant 'Roids, Smash Hits and How Baseball Got Big*. HarperCollins, New York, 2005.

Gene Carney, *Burying the Black Sox: How Baseball's Cover-Up of the 1919 World Series Fix Almost Succeeded*. Potomac Books. Dulles, Virginia, 2006.

Jerrold Casway, *Ed Delahanty and the Emerald Age of Baseball*. University of Notre Dame Press. Notre Dame, Indiana, 2004.

David Cataneo, *Tony C: The Triumph and Tragedy of Tony Conigliaro*. Rutledge Hill Press, Nashville, Tennessee, 1997.

William A. Cook, *The Louisvelle Grays Scandal of 1877: The Taint of Gambling at the Dawn of the National League*. McFarland & Co., Jefferson, North Carolina, 2005.

Robert C. Cottrell, *Blackball, the Black Sox and the Babe: Baseball's Crucial 1920 Season*. McFarland & Co., Inc. Jefferson, North Carolina, 2002.

Robert W. Creamer, *Babe: The Legend Comes to Life*. Simon & Schuster, New York, 1974.

Nicholas Dawidoff, *Baseball: A Literary Anthology*. The Library of America, New York, 2002.

Dennis DeValeria and Jeanne Burke DeValeria, *Honus Wagner: A Biography*. University of Pittsburgh Press, Pittsburgh, Pennsylvania, 1998.

Paul Dickson, *The Dickson Baseball Dictionary*. Facts on File, New York, 1989.

Paul Dickson, *Baseball's Greatest Quotations*. Harper Perennial, New York, 1991.

Perry R. Duis, *The Saloon: Public Drinking in Chicago and Boston, 1880–1920*. University of Illinois Press, Chicago, 1983.

Eric Dunning, *Sport Matters: Sociological Studies of Sports, Violence and Civilization*. Routledge, New York, 1999.

Elizabeth Kandel Englander, *Understanding Violence*. Lawrence Erlbaum Associates, Mahwah, New Jersey, 2003

Bibliography

Paul Gallico, *Farewell to Sport*. A. A. Knopf, New York City, 1944.

John R. Gerdy, *Sports: The All-American Addiction*. University Press of Mississippi, Jackson, Mississippi, 2002.

Daniel E. Ginsburg, *The Fix Is In: A History of Baseball Gambling and Game Fixing Scandals*. McFarland & Company, Inc., Jefferson, North Carolina, 1995.

Avram Goldstein, *Addiction: From Biology to Drug Policy*. Oxford University Press, New York, 2001.

John Steele Gordon, *An Empire of Wealth: The Epic History of American Economic Power*. Harper Collins, New York, 2004.

Ronald Gottesman editor, *Violence in America*. Charles Scribner, New York, 1999.

Stephen Jay Gould, *Triumph and Tragedy in Mudville: A Lifelong Passion for Baseball*. W. W. Norton & Co., New York, 2003.

Marcus Grant and Jorge Litvak, *Drinking Patterns & Their Consequences*. Taylor & Francis, Washington, DC, 1998.

Han Ulrich Gumbrecht, *In Praise of Athletic Beauty*. Harvard University Press, Cambridge, Massachusetts, 2006.

Arthur D. Hittner, *Honus Wagner: The Life of Baseball's "Flying Dutchman."* McFarland & Co., Jefferson, North Carolina, 1996.

Jerome Holtzmann, *The Commissioners: Baseball's Midlife Crisis*. Total Sports, New York, 1998.

Donald Honig, *Baseball When the Grass Was Real: Baseball from the Twenties to the Forties Told by the Men Who Played It*. University of Nebraska Press, Lincoln, Nebraska, 1975.

Neil D. Issacs, *You Bet Your Life: The Burdens of Gambling*. Univ. of Kentucky Press, Lexington, 2001.

Bill James, *Historical Baseball Abstract*. Free Press, New York, 2001.

Matthew Josephson, *The Robber Barons*. Harcourt Brace Jovanovich, New York, 1962.

George B. Kirsch, *Baseball in Blue and Gray*. Princeton University Press, Princeton, New Jersey, 2003.

Maury Klein, *The Life and Legend of Jay Gould*. Johns Hopkins University Press, Baltimore, 1986.

Martin Dinell Kohout, *Hal Chase: The Defiant Life and Turbulent Times of Baseball's Biggest Crook*. McFarland & Co., Jefferson, North Carolina, 2001.

Mark Lamster, *Spalding's World Tour: The Epic Adventure that Took Baseball Around the Globe — And Made It America's Game*. PublicAffairs, New York, 2006.

William Leach, *Land of Desire: Merchants, Power and the Rise of the New American Culture*. Vintage Books, New York, 1993.

Leonard Koppett, *Concise History of Major League Baseball*, Temple University Press, Philadelphia, 1998.

Jackson Lears, *Something for Nothing*. Viking, New York, 2003.

Jon Leizman, *Let's Kill 'Em: Understanding and Controlling Violence in Sports*. University Press of America, New York, 1999.

Mark Edward Lender and James Kirby Martin, *Drinking in America*. The Free Press, New York, 1987.

Peter Levine, *A. G. Spalding and the Rise of Baseball: The Promise of American Sport*. Oxford University Press, New York, 1985.

Michael Lewis, *Moneyball: The Art of Winning an Unfair Game*. W. W. Norton & Co., New York, 2003.

Fred Lieb, *Baseball As I Have Known It*. University of Nebraska Press, Lincoln, Nebraska, 1977.

Michael Mandelbaum, *The Meaning of Sports: Why Americans Watch Baseball, Football, and Basketball and What They See When They Do*. Public Affairs, New York, 2004.

Tom Melville, *Early Baseball and the Rise of the National League*. McFarland & Co., Jefferson, North Carolina, 2001.

Louis Menand, *The Metaphysical Club: A Story of Ideas in America*. Farrar, Straus and Giroux, New York, 2001.

Gregory K. Moffatt, *A Violent Heart: Understanding Aggressive Individuals*. Praeger, Westport, Connecticut, 2002.

John A. Morello, *Selling the President, 1920: Albert D. Lasker, Advertising, and the Election of Warren G. Harding*. Praeger, Westport, Connecticut, 2001.

Peter Morris, *A Game of Inches: The Stories Behind the Innovations that Shaped Baseball*. Ivan R. Dee, Chicago, 2006.

Eugene C. Murdock, *Ban Johnson: Czar of Baseball*. Greenwood Press, Westport, Connecticut, 1982.

David F. Musto, *Drugs in America: A Documentary History*. New York University Press, New York, 2002.

David Nemec, *The Beer & Whiskey League*. Lyons Press, Guilford, Connecticut, 2004.

J. M. D. Olmsted, *Charles-Edouard Brown-Sequard*. The Johns Hopkins Press, Baltimore, 1946.

Jim Orford, *Excessive Appetites: A Psychological View of Addictions*. John Wiley & Sons, Ltd., New York, 2001.

J. Vincent Peterson, Bernard Nisemholz, Gary Robinson, *A Nation Under the Influence: America's Addiction to Alcohol*. Pearson Educational, Boston, 2003.

David Pietrusza, *Judge and Jury: The Life and Times of Judge Kenesaw Mountain Landis*. Diamond Communications, Inc., South Bend, Indiana, 1998.

David Pietrusza, *Rothstein: The Life, Times and Murder of the Criminal Genius Who Fixed the 1919 World Series*. Carroll and Graf, New York, 2003.

Benjamin G. Rader, *Baseball: A History of America's Game*. University of Illinois Press, Chicago, 1992.

Jim Reisler, *Babe Ruth: Launching the Legend*. McGraw Hill, New York, 2004.

James Reston, Jr., *Collision at Home Plate: The Lives of Pete Rose and Bart Giamatti*. University of Nebraska Press, Lincoln, Nebraska, 1997.

Steven A. Riess, *Major Problems in American Sport History*. Houghton Mifflin Co., Boston, 1997.

Steven A. Riess, *Touching Base: Professional Baseball and American Culture in the Progressive Era* University of Illinois Press, Chicago, 1999.

Steven A. Riess, *Sport in Industrial America*. Harlan Davidson, Wheeling, Illinois, 1995.

Lawrence S. Ritter, *The Glory of Their Times: The Story of the Early Days of Baseball Told by the Men Who Played It*. William Morrow, New York, 1981.

Pete Rose, *My Prison Without Bars*. Rodale, New York, 2004.

John P. Rossi, *The National Game: Baseball and American Culture*. Ivan R. Dee, Chicago, 2000.

Philip Seib, *The Player: Christy Matthewson, Baseball and the American Century*. Four Walls Eight Windows, New York, 2003.

Rebecca Shannonhouse, *Under the Influence: The Literature of Addiction*. Modern Library, New York, 2003.

Richard Scheinen, *Field of Screams: The Dark Underside of America's National Pastime*. W. W. Norton & Co., New York, 1994.

Harold Seymour, *Baseball: The Early Years*. Oxford University Press, New York, 1960.

Harold Seymour, *Baseball: The Golden Age*. Oxford University Press, New York, 1971.

Rebecca Shannonhouse, *Under the Influence: The Literature of Addiction*. Modern Library, New York, 2003.

James C. Simmons, *Star-Spangled Eden: 19th Century America through the Eyes of Dickens, Wilde, Frances Trollope, Frank Harry and Other British Travelers*. Carroll and Graf, New York, 2000.

Tom Simon, *Deadball Stars of the National League*. Brassey's Inc., Washington, DC, 2004.

Richard Skolnick, *Baseball and the Pursuit of Innocence: A Fresh Look at the Old Ball Game*. Texas A & M University Press, College Station, Texas, 1994.

Burt Solomon, *Where They Ain't: The Fabled Life and Untimely Death of the Original Baltimore Orioles, the Team That Gave Birth to Modern Baseball*. The Free Press, New York, 1999.

Mike Sowell, *The Pitch That Killed*. MacMillan Publishing Co., New York, 1989.

Albert Spalding, *America's National Game: Historic Facts Concerning the Beginning, Evolution, Development and Popularity of Baseball*. University of Nebraska Press, Lincoln, Nebraska, 1992.

J. G. Taylor Spink, *Judge Landis and 25 Years of Baseball*. Thomas Y. Crowell Co., New York, 1947.

Al Stump, *Cobb: A Biography*. Algonquin Books, Chapel Hill, North Carolina, 1994.

Alan Trachtenberg, *The Incorporation of America: Culture & Society in the Gilded Age*. Hill & Wang, New York, 1982.

Jules Tygiel, *Past Time: Baseball as History*. Oxford University Press, New York, 2000.

David Q. Voigt, *American Baseball: From a Gentlemen's Sport to the Commissioner System*. Pennsylvania State University Press, University Park, Pennsylvania, 1983.

Michael B. Walker, *The Psychology of Gambling*. Pergamon Press, New York, 1992.

Geoffrey C. Ward and Ken Burns, *Baseball: An Illustrated History*. Alfred A. Knopf, New York, 1994.

Harvey Wasserman, *Harvey Wasserman's History of the United States*. Perennial Library, New York, 1972.

David Wells, *Perfect I'm Not: Boomer on Beer, Brawls, Backaches, and Baseball*. William Morrow, New York, 2003.

Deanne Westbrook, *Ground Rules: Baseball & Myth*. University of Illinois Press, Chicago, 1996.

Robert H. Wiebe, *The Search for Order: 1877–1920*. Hill and Wang, New York, 1967.

Andrew Zimbalist, *May the Best Team Win: Baseball Economics and Public Policy*. Brookings Institution Press, Washington, DC, 2003.

Index